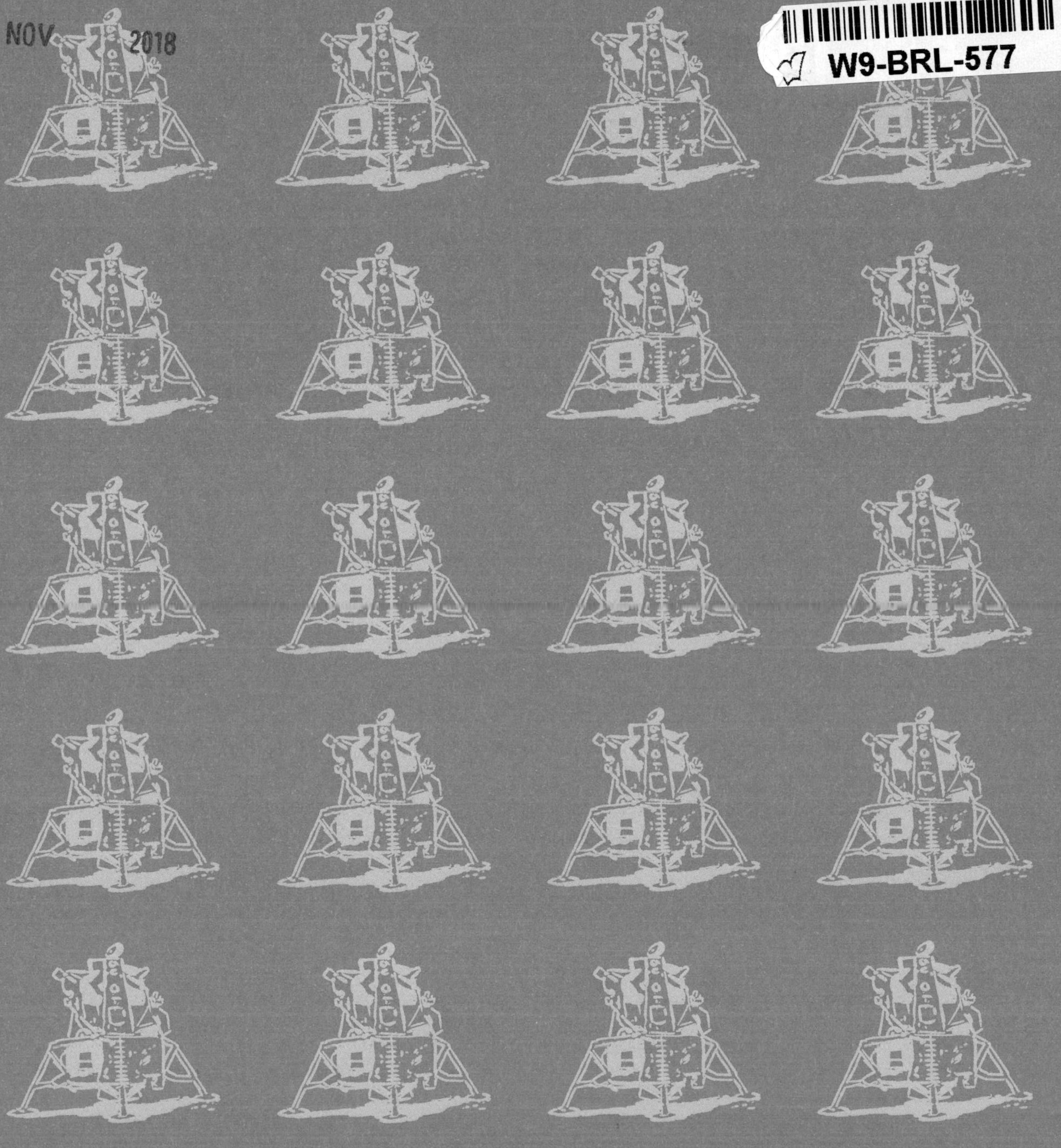

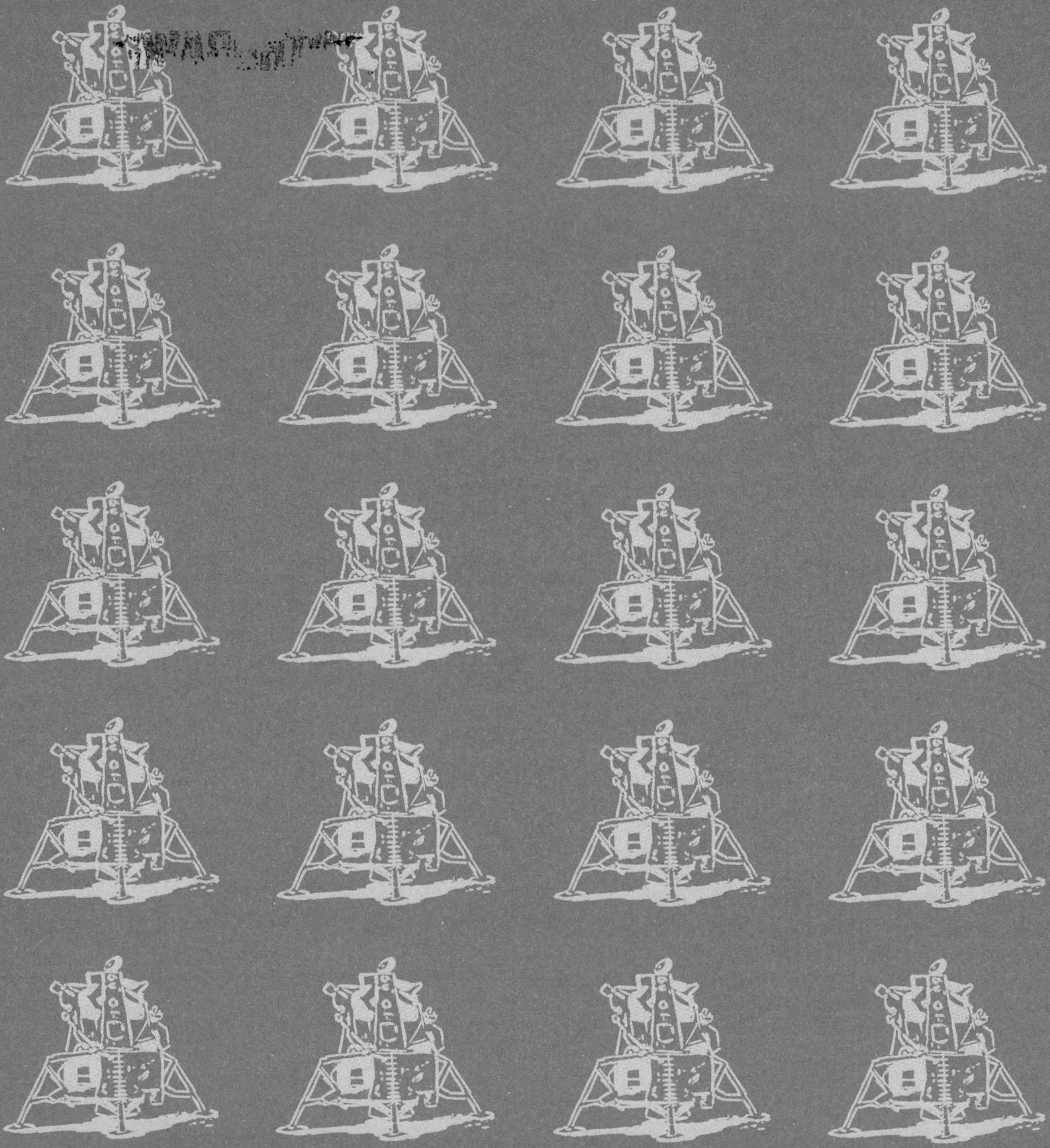

ORDINARY PEOPLE CHANGE the WORLD

I am Neil Armstrong

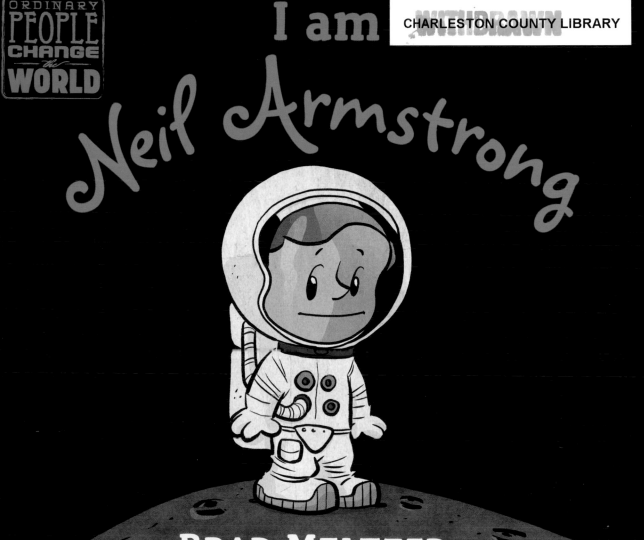

BRAD MELTZER

illustrated by Christopher Eliopoulos

 DIAL BOOKS FOR YOUNG READERS

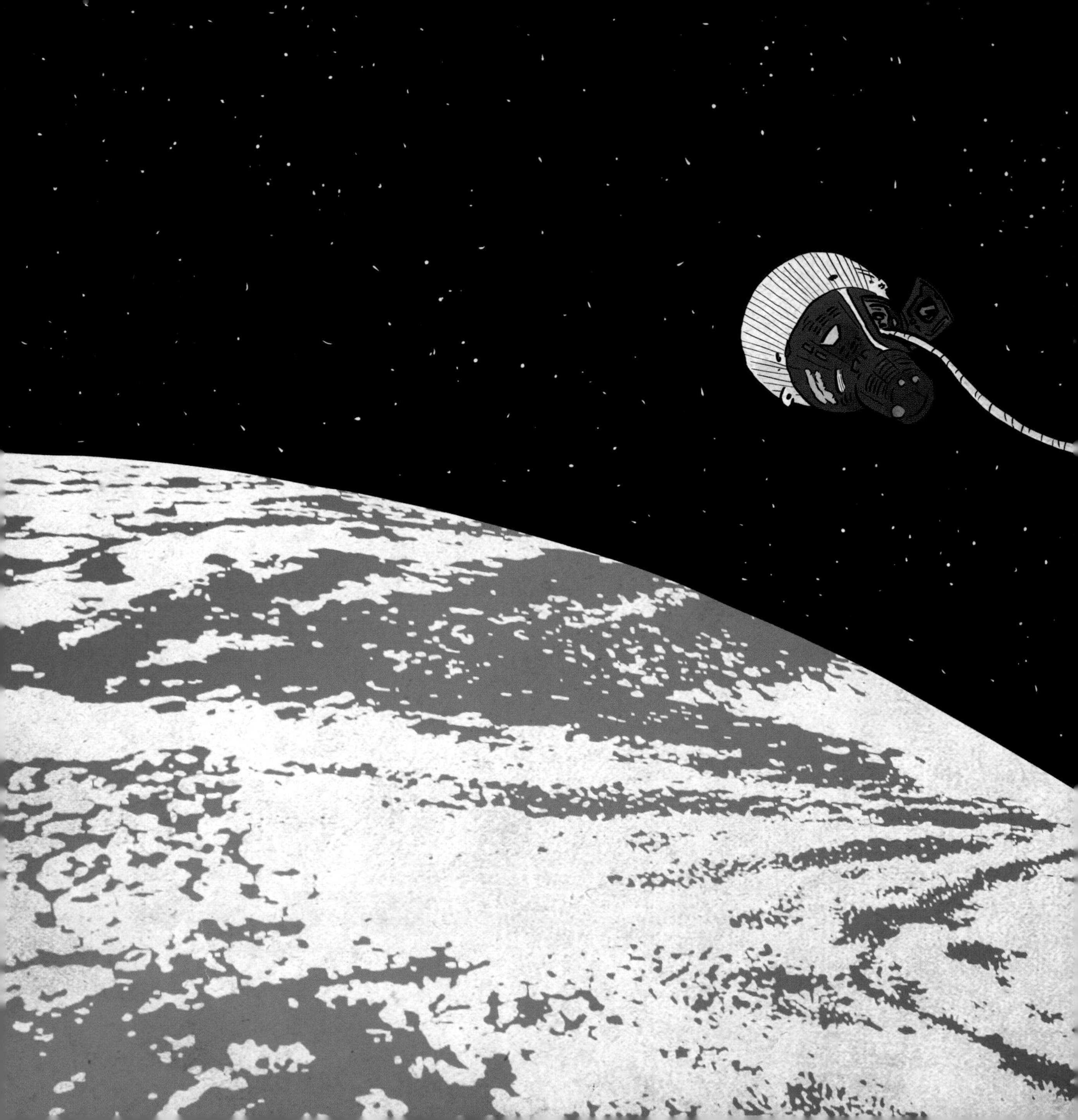

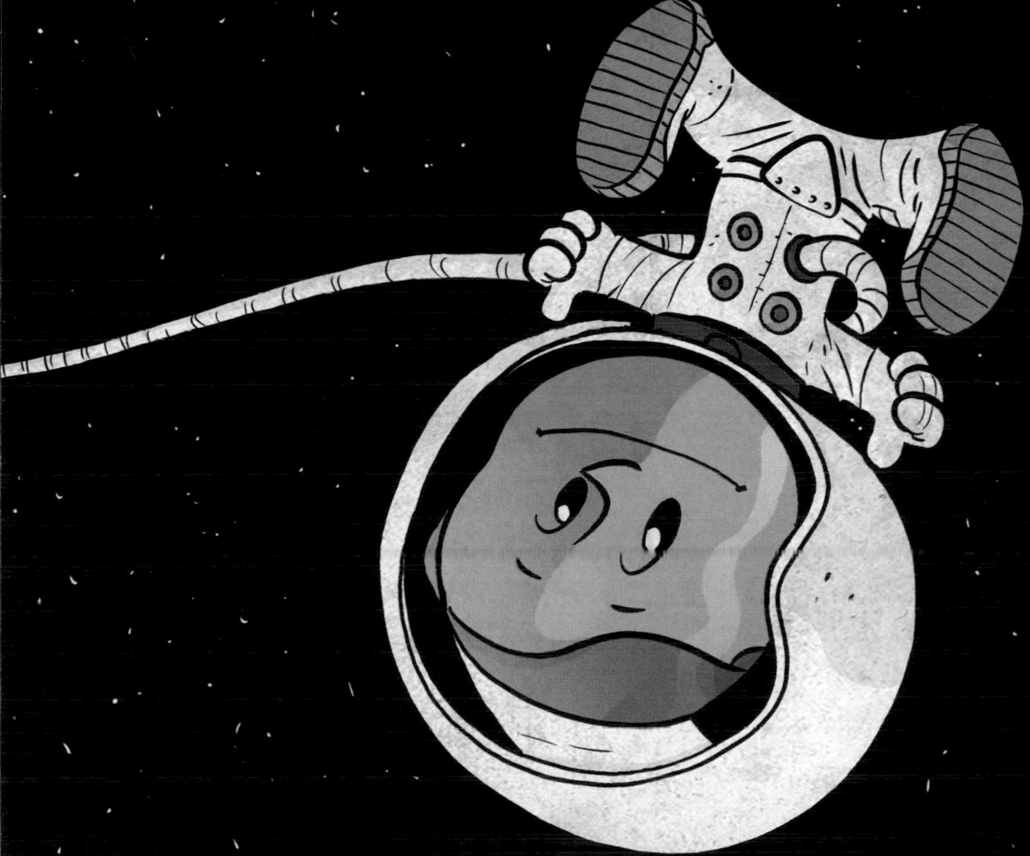

I am **Neil Armstrong.**

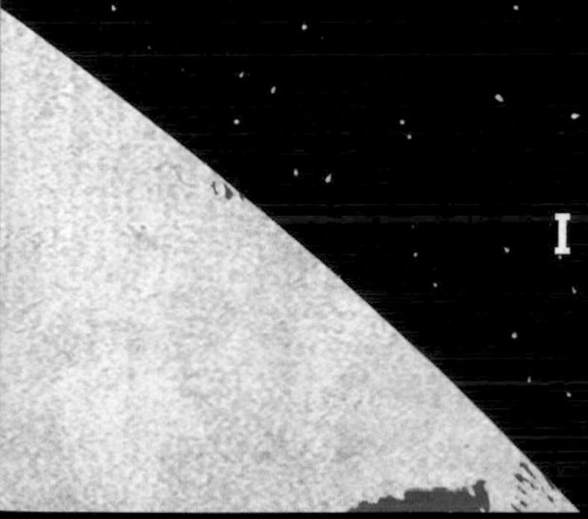

I grew up on a farm with no electricity.
When I was eight years old, my goal was to climb this silver maple tree—the biggest one in my backyard.

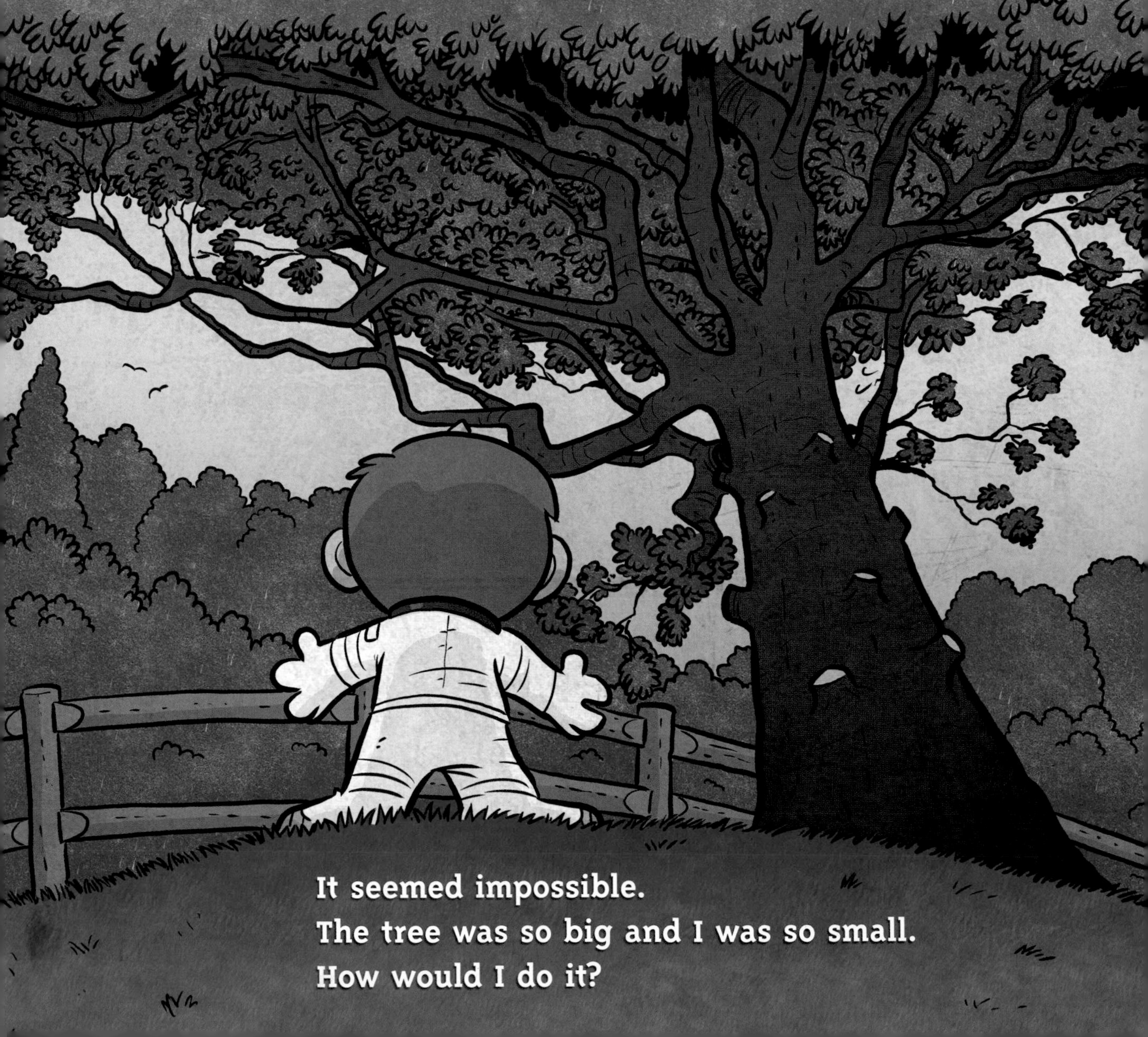

It seemed impossible.
The tree was so big and I was so small.
How would I do it?

I'd need to be brave. I wasn't a brave kid, though.

Back in Ohio, when I was three years old, I got scared when we went to see Santa Claus.

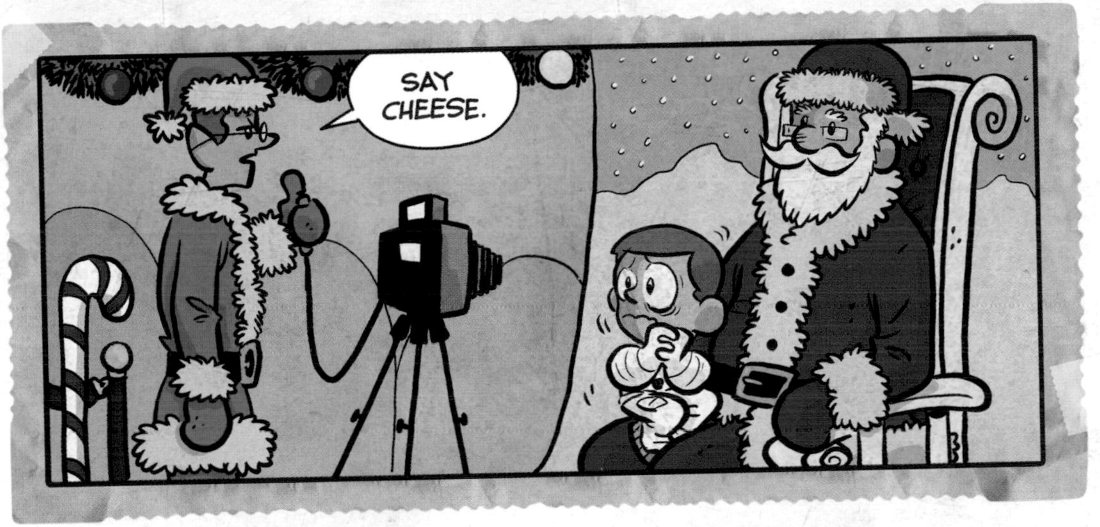
SAY CHEESE.

I'd also need to be smart.

As a kid, I loved to read.

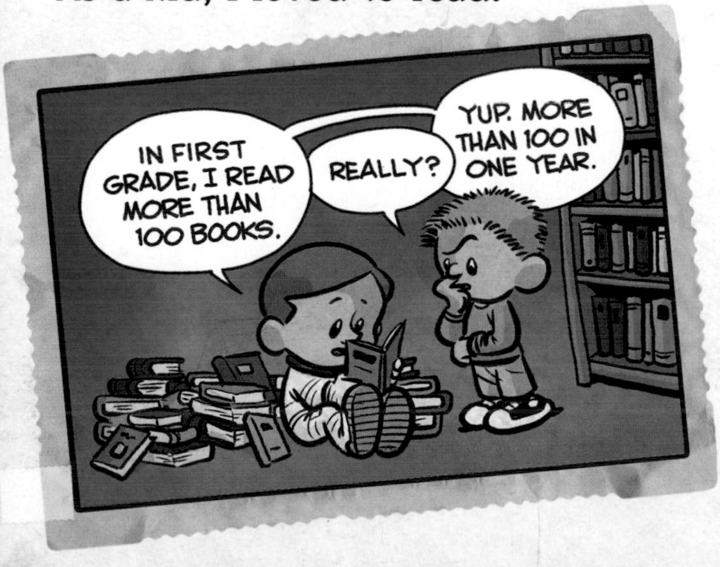
IN FIRST GRADE, I READ MORE THAN 100 BOOKS.
REALLY?
YUP. MORE THAN 100 IN ONE YEAR.

Finally, I'd need to be patient.

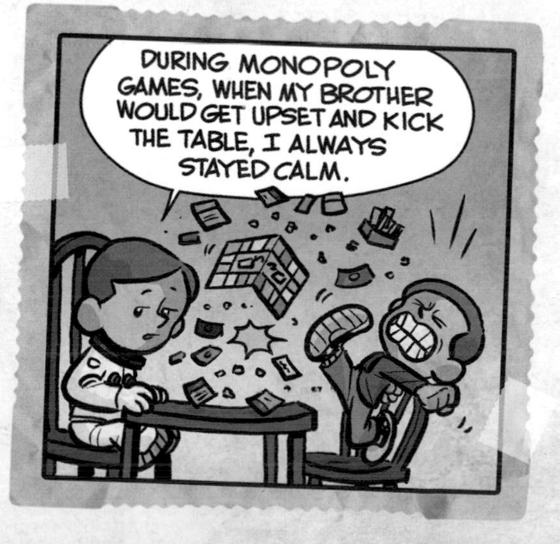
DURING MONOPOLY GAMES, WHEN MY BROTHER WOULD GET UPSET AND KICK THE TABLE, I ALWAYS STAYED CALM.

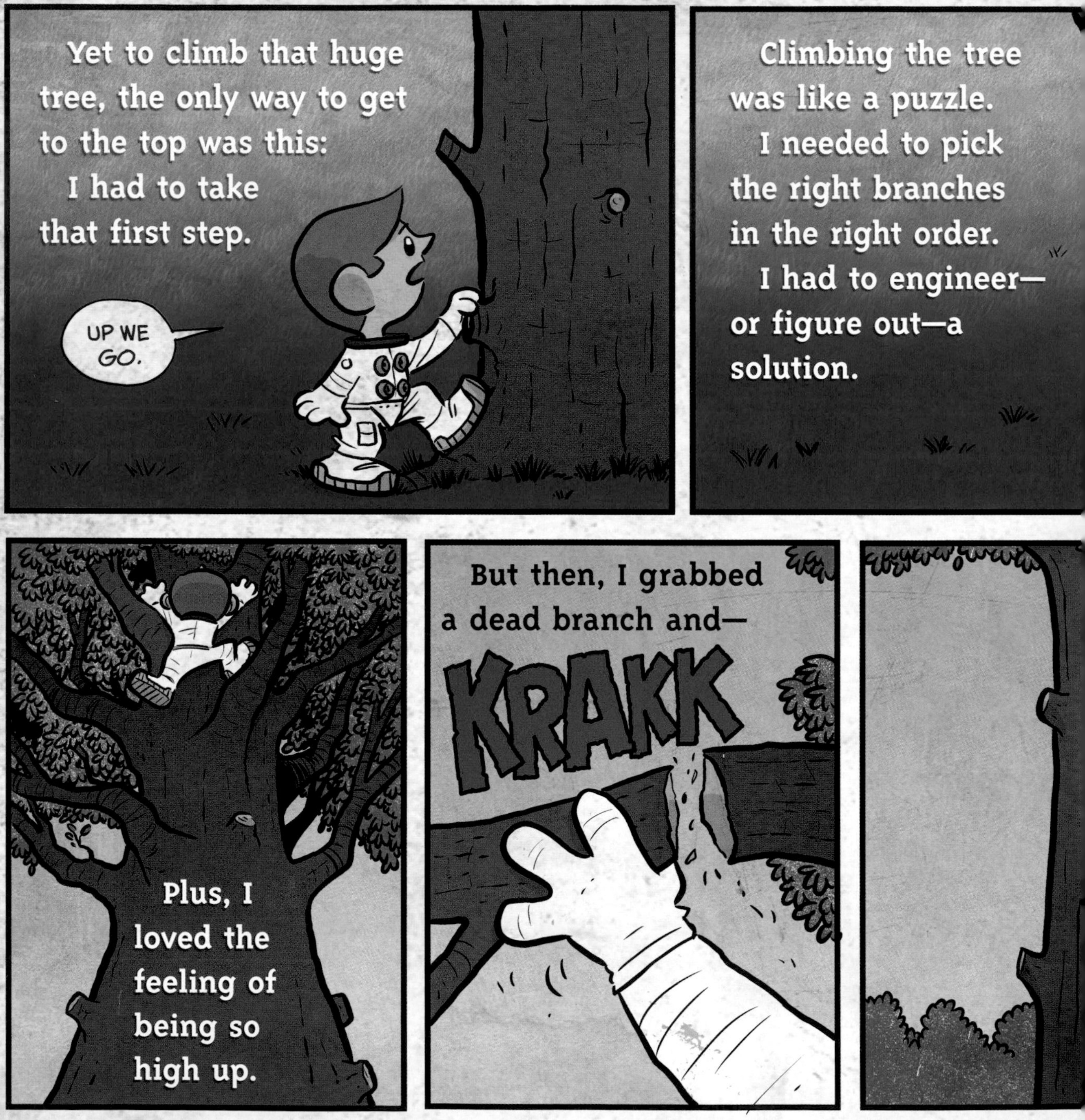
Yet to climb that huge tree, the only way to get to the top was this:
I had to take that first step.
UP WE GO.
Climbing the tree was like a puzzle.
I needed to pick the right branches in the right order.
I had to engineer—or figure out—a solution.
Plus, I loved the feeling of being so high up.
But then, I grabbed a dead branch and—
KRAKK

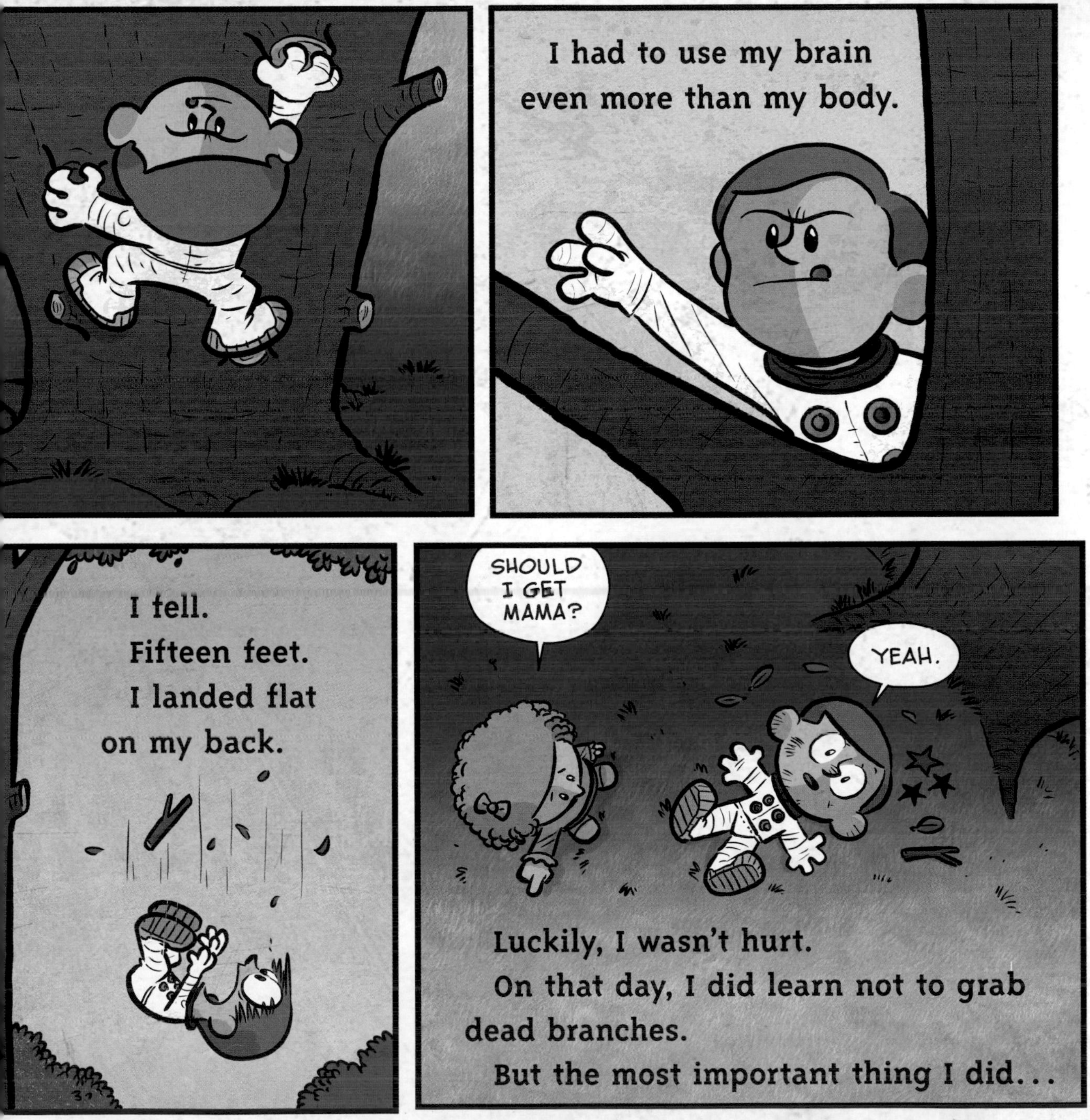
I had to use my brain
even more than my body.
I fell.
Fifteen feet.
I landed flat
on my back.
SHOULD I GET MAMA?
YEAH.
Luckily, I wasn't hurt.
On that day, I did learn not to grab
dead branches.
But the most important thing I did...

. . .was get back up again.

Success never comes easily. It takes hard work.

And when it came to hard work, I was really good at that.

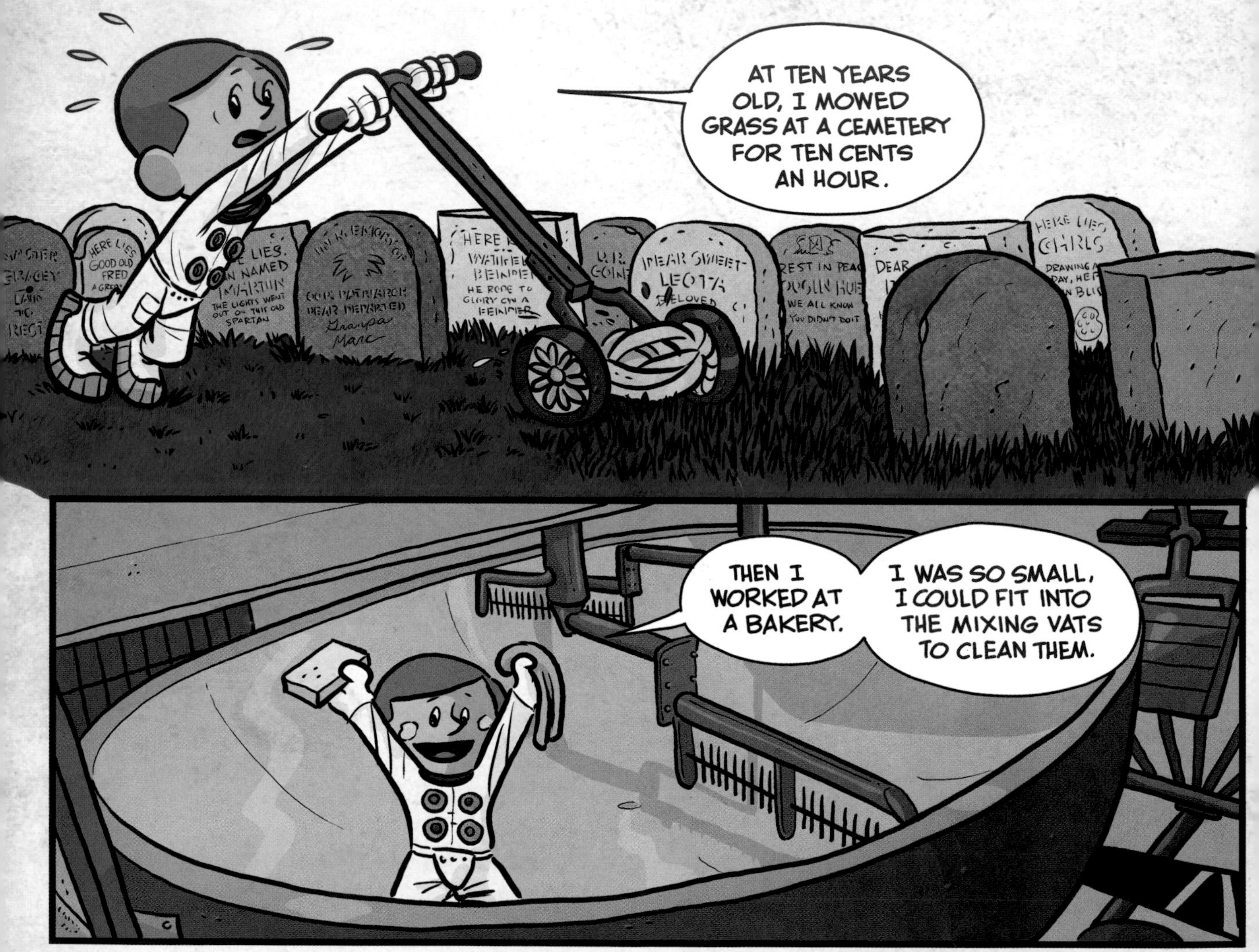
AT TEN YEARS OLD, I MOWED GRASS AT A CEMETERY FOR TEN CENTS AN HOUR.
HERE LIES GOOD OLD FRED
DEAR SWEET LEOTA
HERE LIES CHRIS
THEN I WORKED AT A BAKERY.
I WAS SO SMALL, I COULD FIT INTO THE MIXING VATS TO CLEAN THEM.

Those jobs helped pay for the one thing I loved more than anything else.

Airplanes.

My mom bought me my first toy plane when I was two or three years old.

After that, I was always zooming around the house and through the neighborhood.

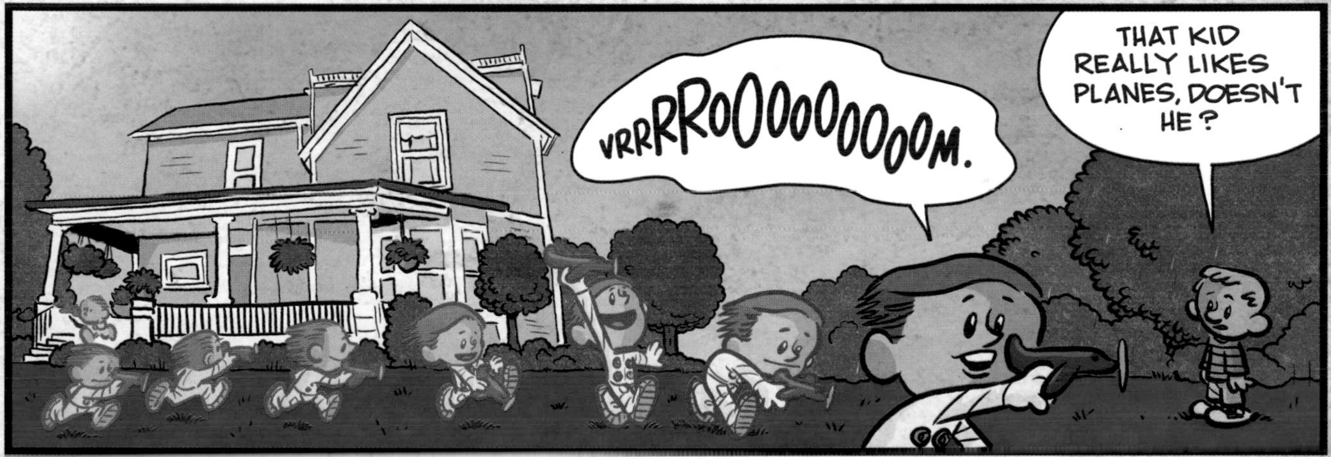
VRRRROOOOOOOOOOM.
THAT KID REALLY LIKES PLANES, DOESN'T HE?

When I was six, I took my first real airplane ride in an aluminum high-wing monoplane called the *Tin Goose*.

The twelve seats inside were all wicker chairs. It rattled like crazy!

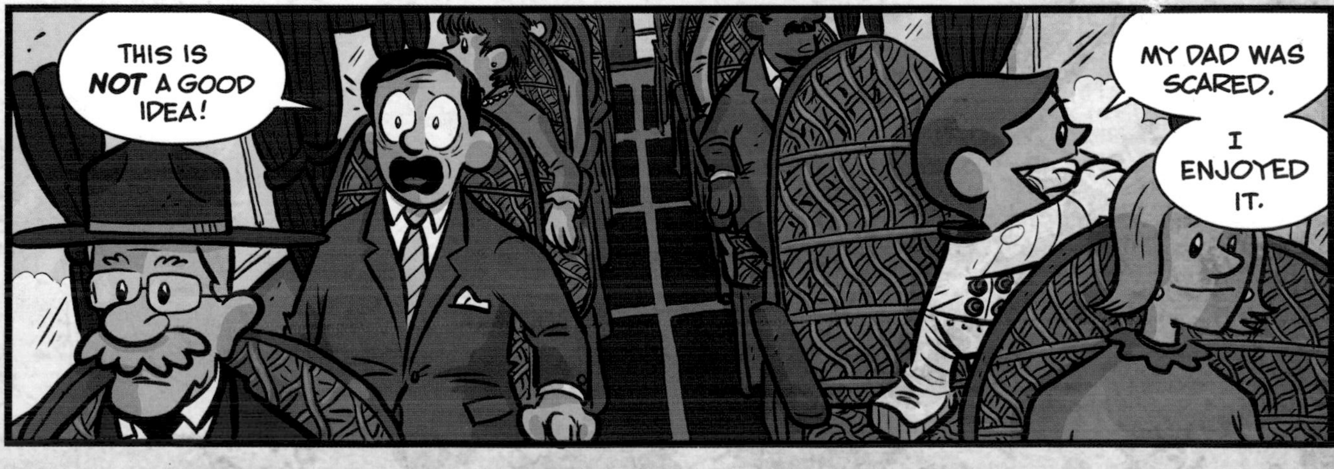
THIS IS **NOT** A GOOD IDEA!
MY DAD WAS SCARED.
I ENJOYED IT.

I became obsessed with learning about planes, reading about them, and even building them.

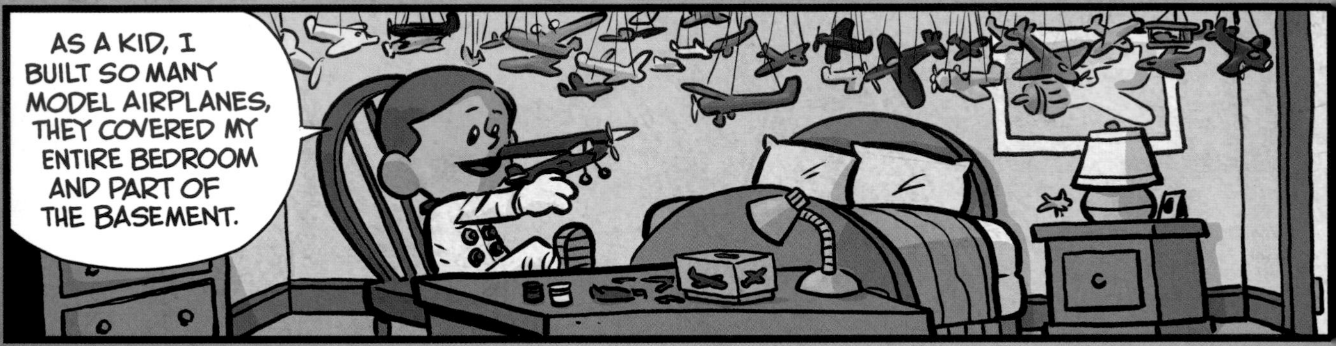

AS A KID, I BUILT SO MANY MODEL AIRPLANES, THEY COVERED MY ENTIRE BEDROOM AND PART OF THE BASEMENT.

By the time I was fifteen, instead of buying toy airplanes, I started saving my money for flying lessons.

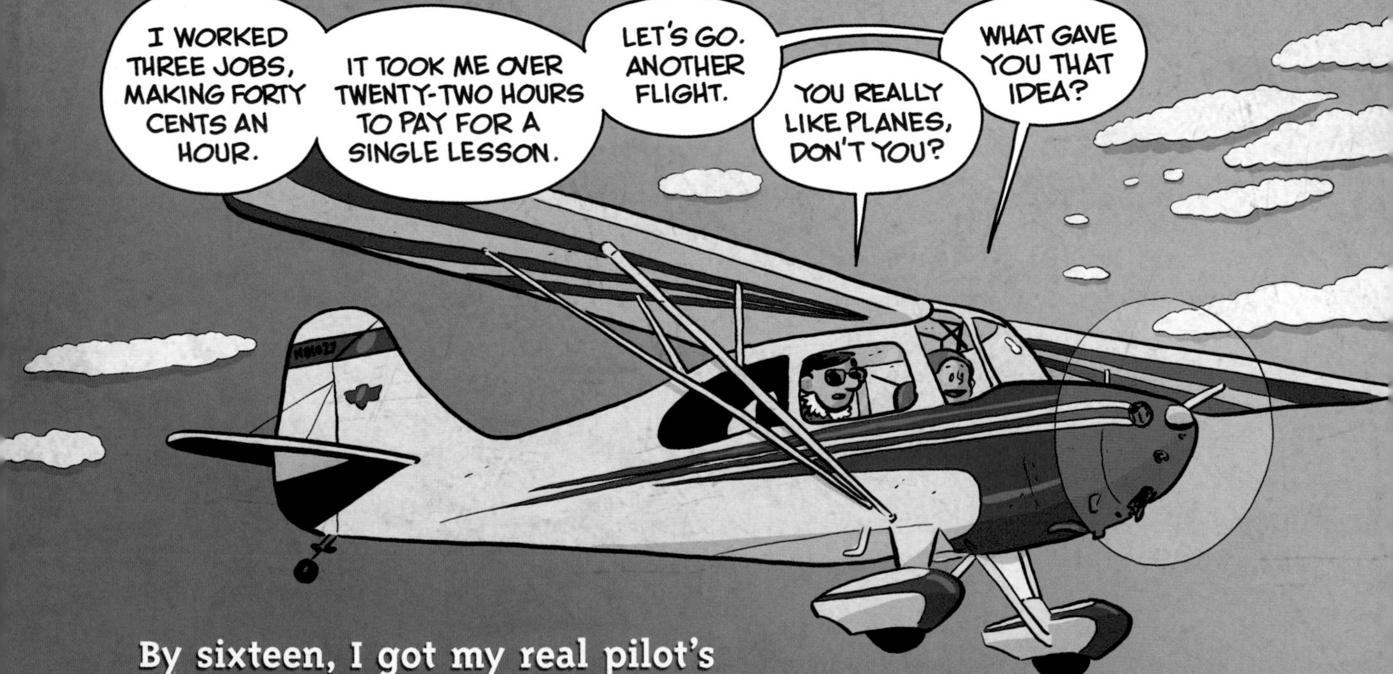

I WORKED THREE JOBS, MAKING FORTY CENTS AN HOUR.
IT TOOK ME OVER TWENTY-TWO HOURS TO PAY FOR A SINGLE LESSON.
LET'S GO. ANOTHER FLIGHT.
YOU REALLY LIKE PLANES, DON'T YOU?
WHAT GAVE YOU THAT IDEA?

By sixteen, I got my real pilot's license—even before I got my driver's license.

As a teenager, I loved flying so much, I'd have the same dream over and over.

In the dream, by holding my breath I could hover over the ground.

I didn't fly or really move. I'd just float there.

When I got older, I joined the navy, flying in seventy-eight missions during the Korean War.

On one of them, my plane lost its wing, so I needed to eject and get out immediately.

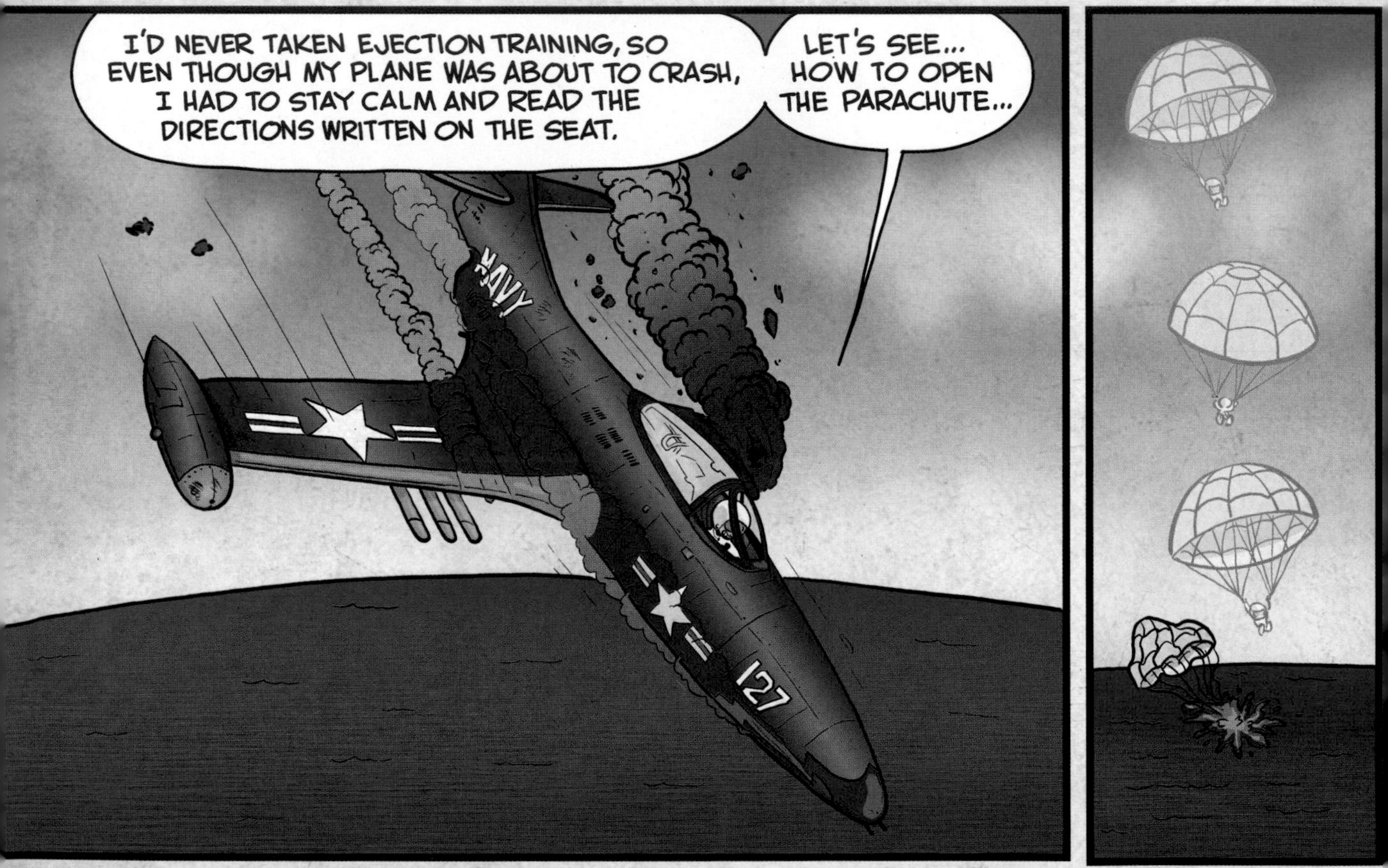
I'D NEVER TAKEN EJECTION TRAINING, SO EVEN THOUGH MY PLANE WAS ABOUT TO CRASH, I HAD TO STAY CALM AND READ THE DIRECTIONS WRITTEN ON THE SEAT.
LET'S SEE... HOW TO OPEN THE PARACHUTE...
NAVY
127

I landed safely in the water.

By the end of the war, the U.S. gave me many war medals, though I never bragged about them. I'd been taught to stay humble.

In college, I studied how to be an engineer, which is a person who designs and builds machines and structures.

That love of engineering led me to become a test pilot.

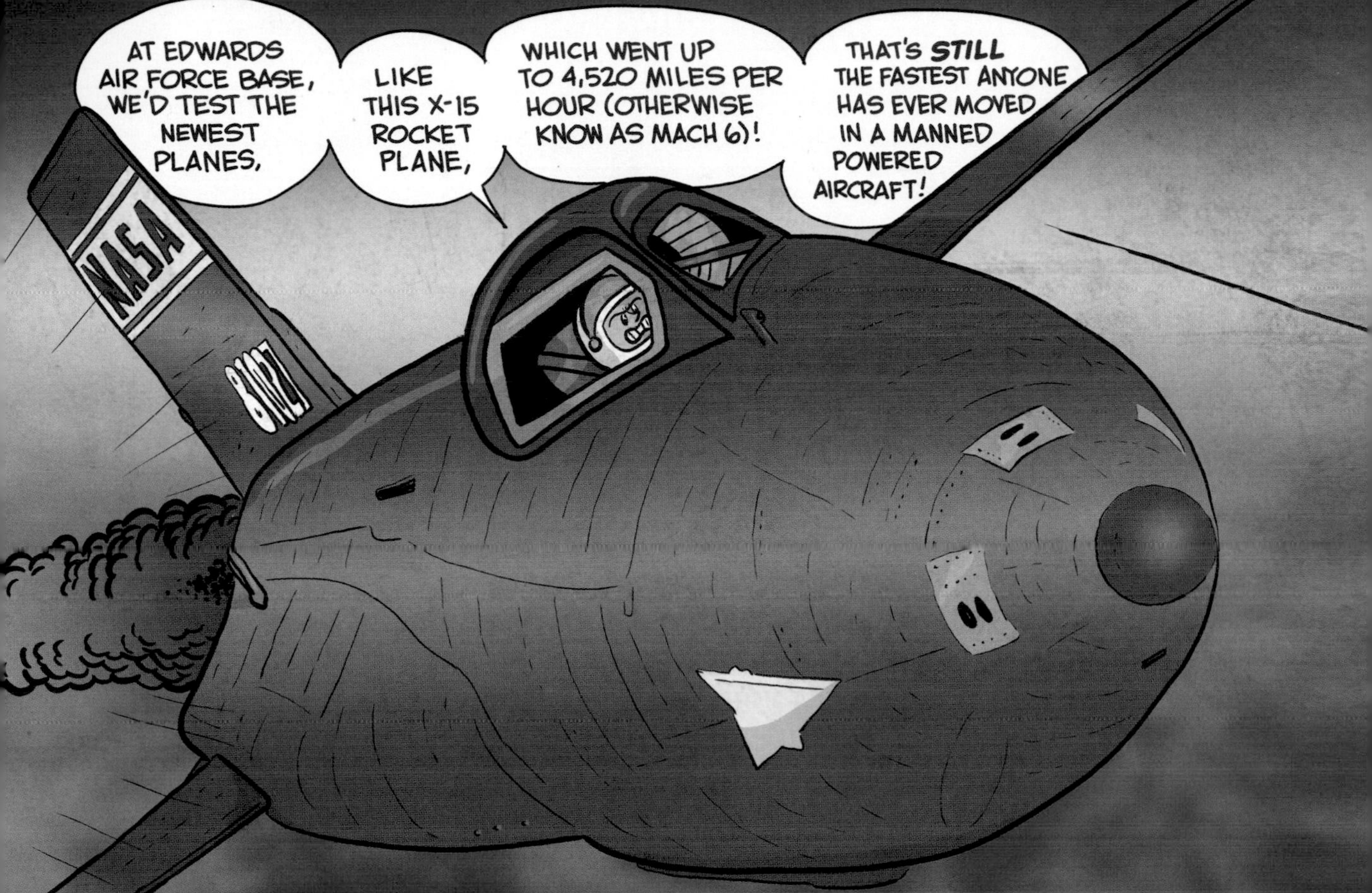

AT EDWARDS AIR FORCE BASE, WE'D TEST THE NEWEST PLANES,
LIKE THIS X-15 ROCKET PLANE,
WHICH WENT UP TO 4,520 MILES PER HOUR (OTHERWISE KNOW AS MACH 6)!
THAT'S **STILL** THE FASTEST ANYONE HAS EVER MOVED IN A MANNED POWERED AIRCRAFT!
NASA

Engineers test and learn, test and learn.

By flying that rocket, we learned new things about aerodynamics (how air affects a plane), hypersonic speed, and the best materials to use on airplanes.

Making things better—that's engineering!

In 1957, the "space race" had begun.

Both America and the Soviet Union were competing to be the first into outer space.

The Soviets sent the first satellite into space. It was named Sputnik.

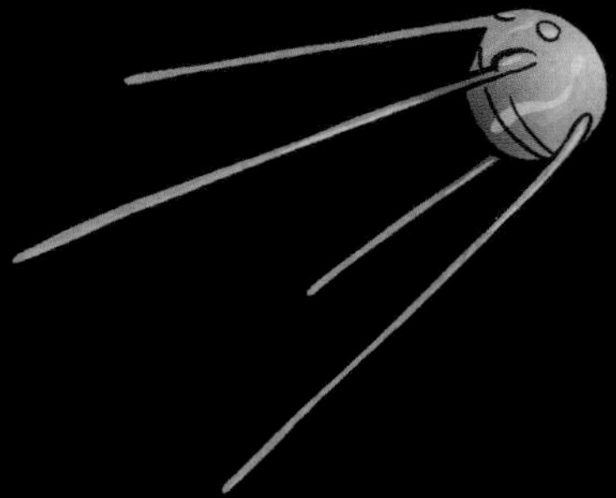

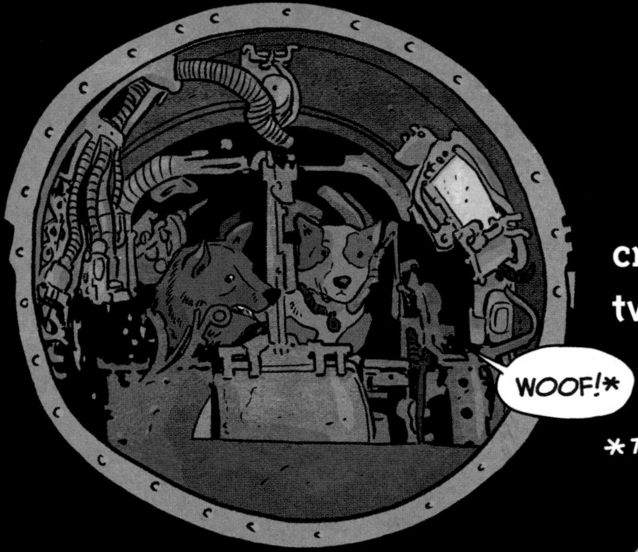
WOOF!*

Then they sent the first living creatures that survived space travel: two dogs named Strelka and Belka.

*TRANSLATION: WE GOT BACK SAFELY.

The Soviet Union also sent the first human, Yuri Gagarin, into space, though we sent a person named Alan Shepard soon after.

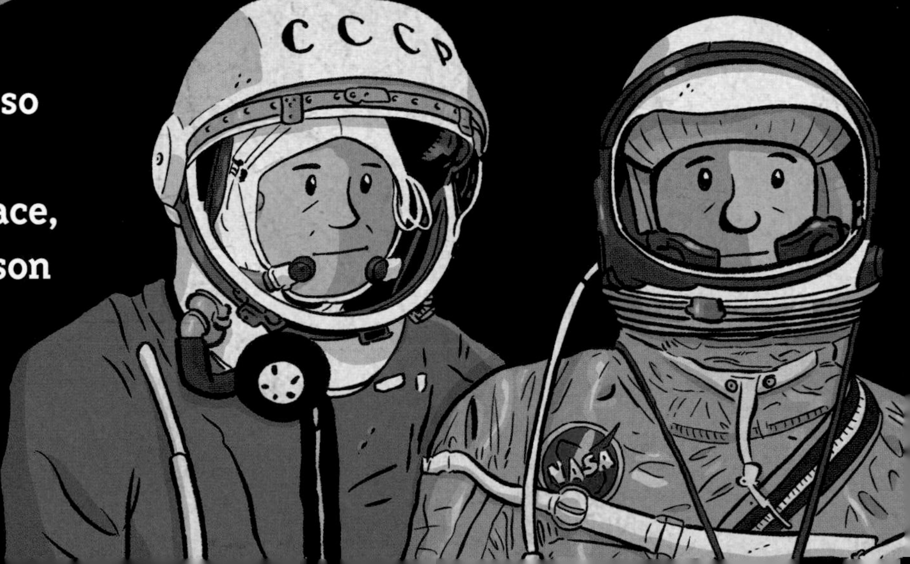
CCCP
NASA

America wanted to catch up, so President John F. Kennedy Jr. issued a challenge that year.

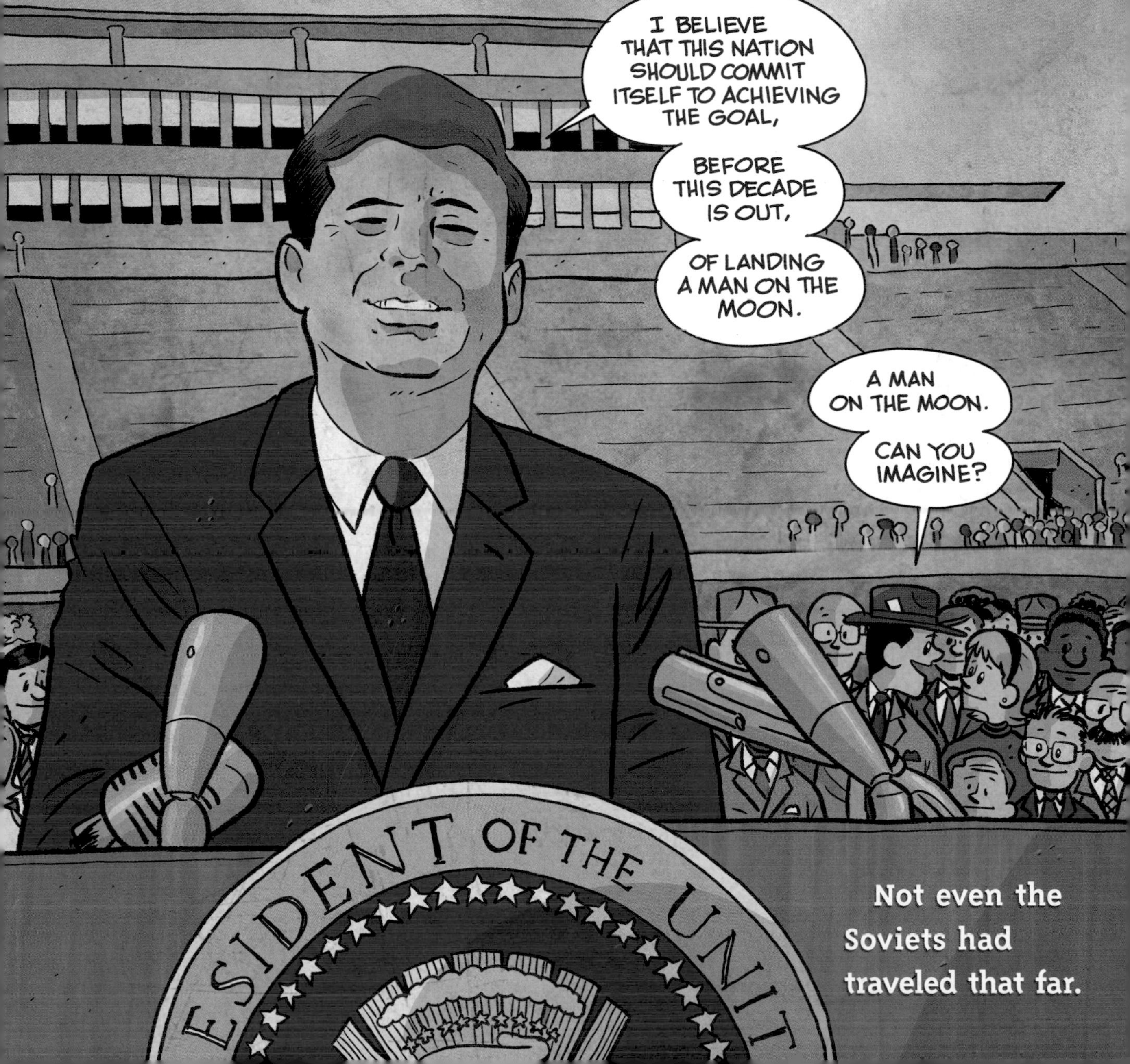
I BELIEVE THAT THIS NATION SHOULD COMMIT ITSELF TO ACHIEVING THE GOAL,
BEFORE THIS DECADE IS OUT,
OF LANDING A MAN ON THE MOON.
A MAN ON THE MOON.
CAN YOU IMAGINE?
ESIDENT OF THE UNIT

Not even the Soviets had traveled that far.

So how would we manage to climb that high?

The only thing we knew for sure was this: We'd have to engineer a solution.

We needed new ideas. New equipment.

And, to fly all the way to the moon—we needed a new type of pilot: an astronaut!

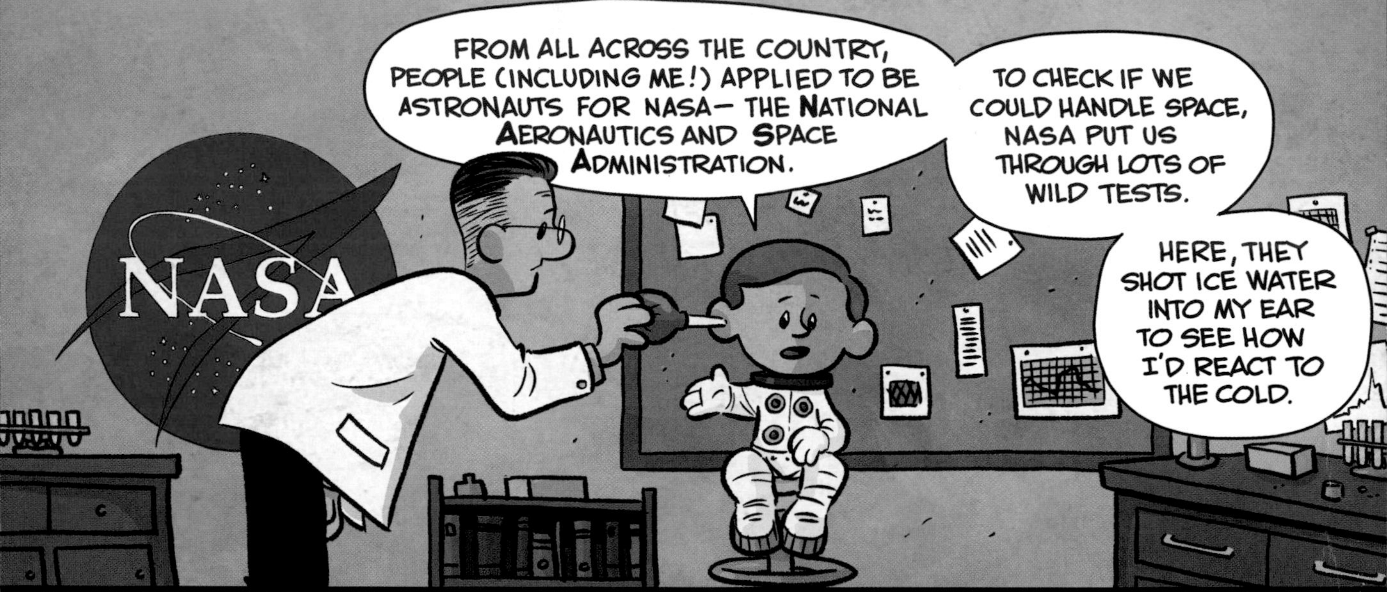

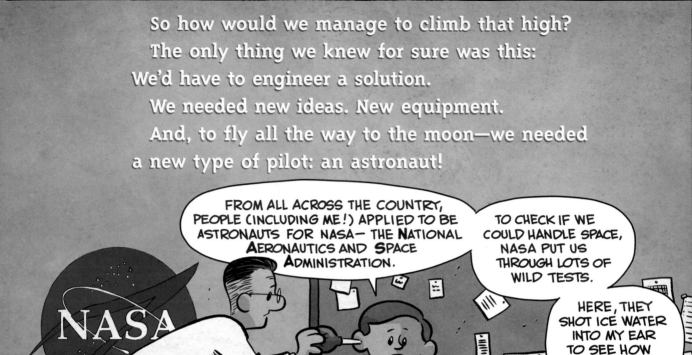

FROM ALL ACROSS THE COUNTRY, PEOPLE (INCLUDING ME!) APPLIED TO BE ASTRONAUTS FOR NASA— THE NATIONAL AERONAUTICS AND SPACE ADMINISTRATION.
TO CHECK IF WE COULD HANDLE SPACE, NASA PUT US THROUGH LOTS OF WILD TESTS.
HERE, THEY SHOT ICE WATER INTO MY EAR TO SEE HOW I'D REACT TO THE COLD.
NASA

In another test, they put me in a black room—no lights, no clocks—and told me to come out after two hours.

They were testing if we could judge time without tools.

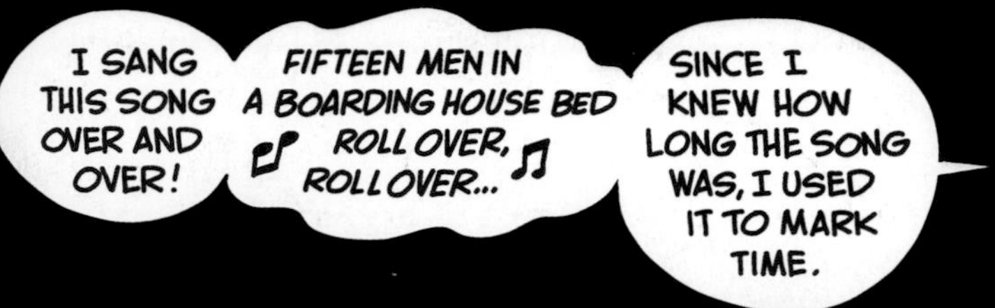

I SANG THIS SONG OVER AND OVER!
FIFTEEN MEN IN A BOARDING HOUSE BED ROLL OVER, ROLL OVER...
SINCE I KNEW HOW LONG THE SONG WAS, I USED IT TO MARK TIME.

They even put me in a really hot room, where it got up to 145 degrees Fahrenheit.

To keep my body heat normal, I did nothing but sit still.

I tried to not even think.

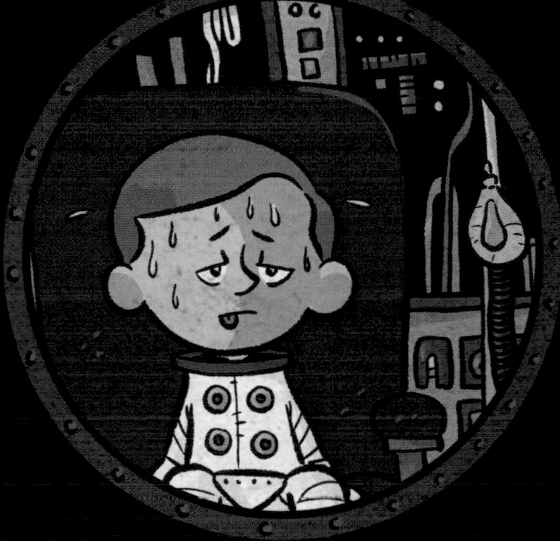

And of course, they spun me around and around and around.

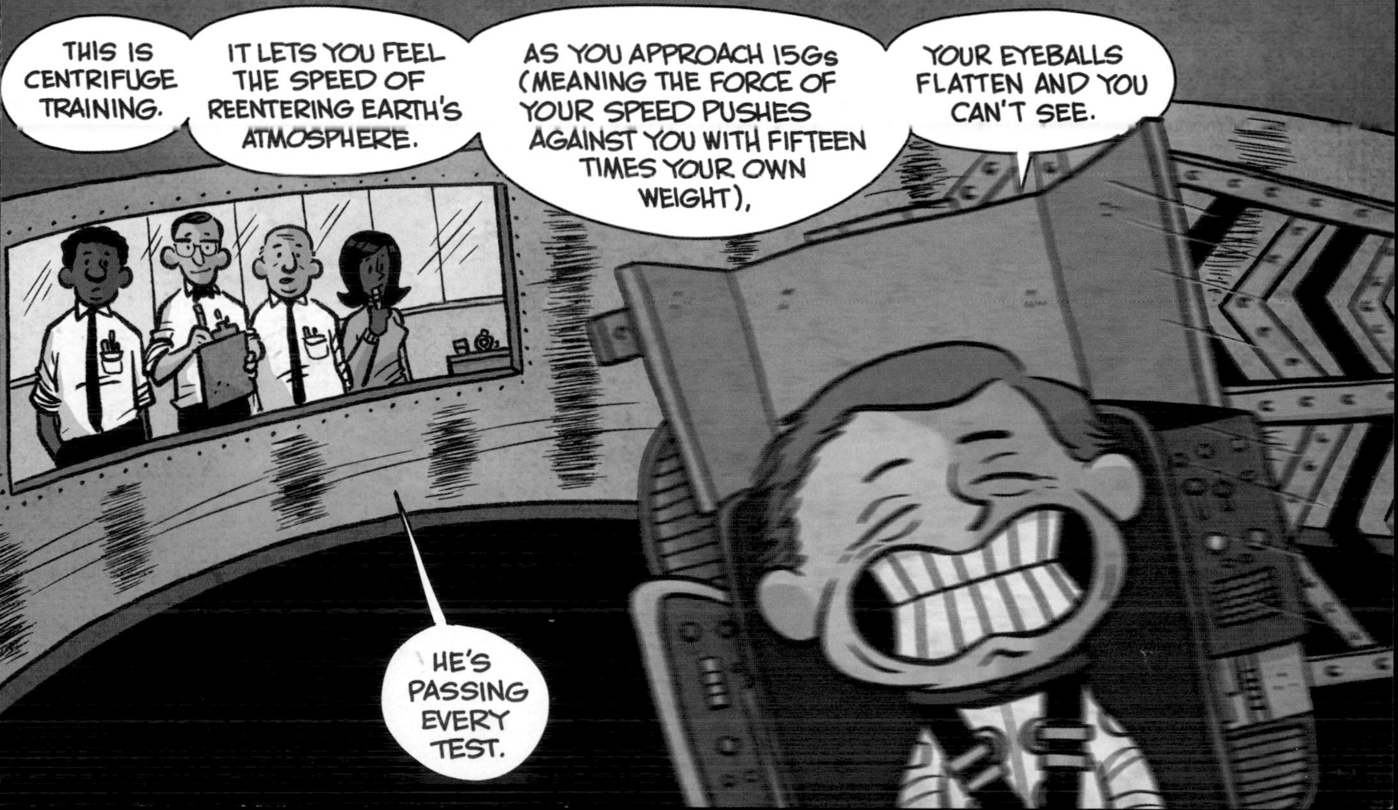
THIS IS CENTRIFUGE TRAINING.
IT LETS YOU FEEL THE SPEED OF REENTERING EARTH'S ATMOSPHERE.
AS YOU APPROACH 15Gs (MEANING THE FORCE OF YOUR SPEED PUSHES AGAINST YOU WITH FIFTEEN TIMES YOUR OWN WEIGHT),
YOUR EYEBALLS FLATTEN AND YOU CAN'T SEE.
HE'S PASSING EVERY TEST.

To get to the moon, NASA had a step-by-step plan.
The Mercury missions would take Americans into space.
And the Gemini missions would take us into orbit around the Earth.
With each step, we would get a little farther, and go a little higher.

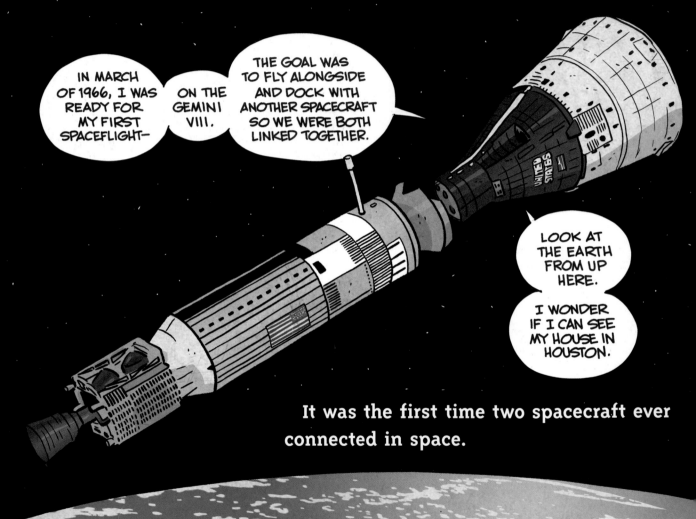

IN MARCH OF 1966, I WAS READY FOR MY FIRST SPACEFLIGHT—

ON THE GEMINI VIII.

THE GOAL WAS TO FLY ALONGSIDE AND DOCK WITH ANOTHER SPACECRAFT SO WE WERE BOTH LINKED TOGETHER.

LOOK AT THE EARTH FROM UP HERE.

I WONDER IF I CAN SEE MY HOUSE IN HOUSTON.

It was the first time two spacecraft ever connected in space.

Everyone started celebrating the moment we were docked.

And then, suddenly, we were undocked again and spinning out of control.

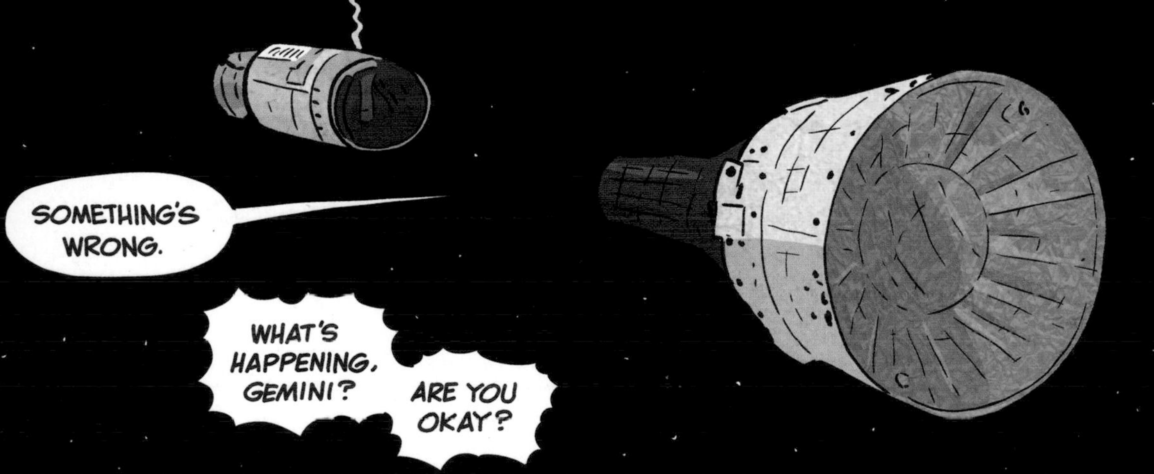
SOMETHING'S WRONG.
WHAT'S HAPPENING, GEMINI?
ARE YOU OKAY?

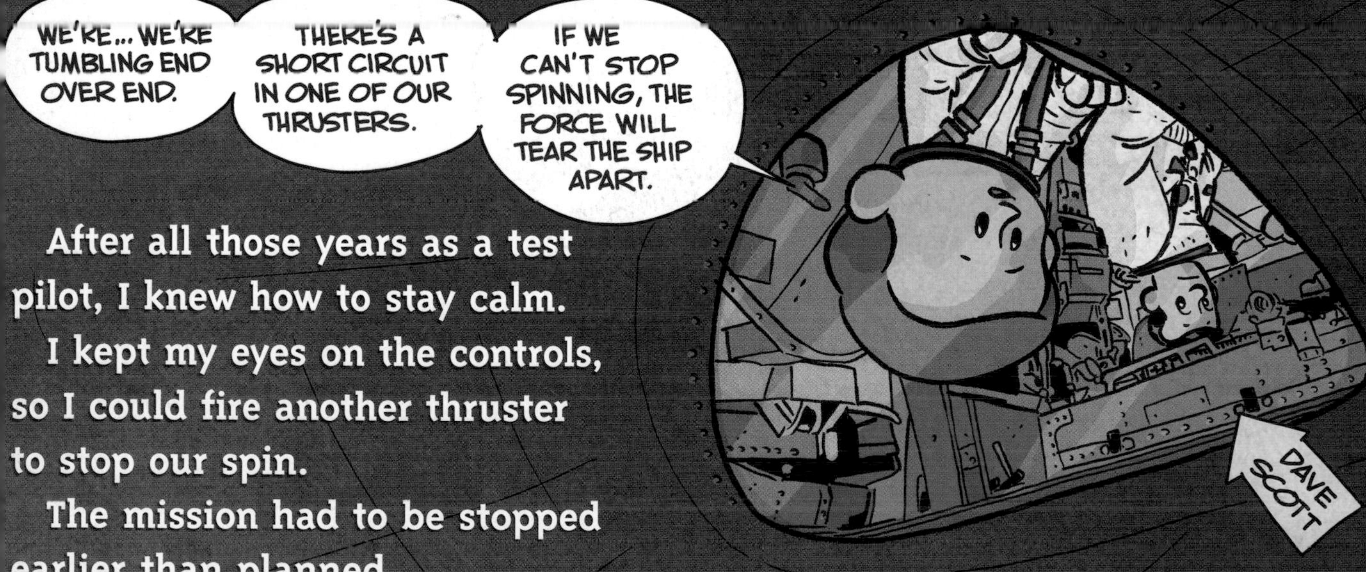
WE'RE... WE'RE TUMBLING END OVER END.
THERE'S A SHORT CIRCUIT IN ONE OF OUR THRUSTERS.
IF WE CAN'T STOP SPINNING, THE FORCE WILL TEAR THE SHIP APART.
DAVE SCOTT

After all those years as a test pilot, I knew how to stay calm.

I kept my eyes on the controls, so I could fire another thruster to stop our spin.

The mission had to be stopped earlier than planned.

We landed safely, but it taught me another lesson.

Nothing in space is easy.

Over and over, there were setbacks and devastating crashes.

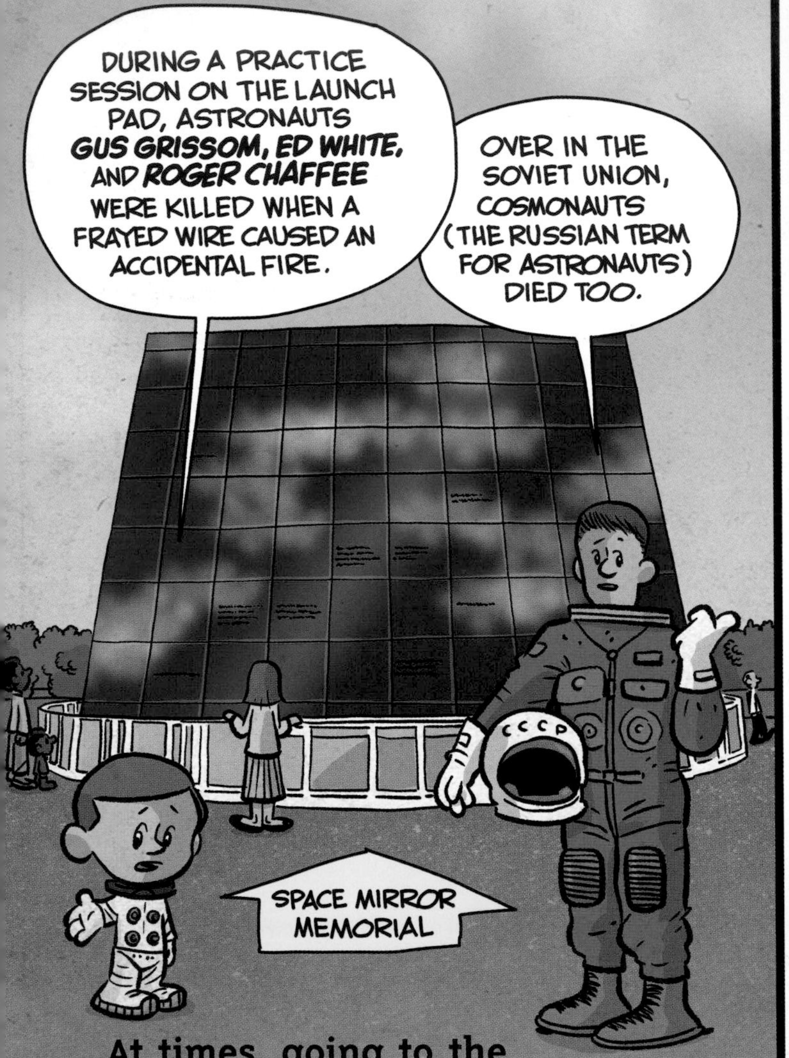
DURING A PRACTICE SESSION ON THE LAUNCH PAD, ASTRONAUTS **GUS GRISSOM, ED WHITE,** AND **ROGER CHAFFEE** WERE KILLED WHEN A FRAYED WIRE CAUSED AN ACCIDENTAL FIRE.
OVER IN THE SOVIET UNION, COSMONAUTS (THE RUSSIAN TERM FOR ASTRONAUTS) DIED TOO.
CCCP
SPACE MIRROR MEMORIAL

At times, going to the moon seemed impossible.

But we never let it stop us.

With each setback, we learned how to strengthen the Apollo spacecraft, which would take us to the moon.

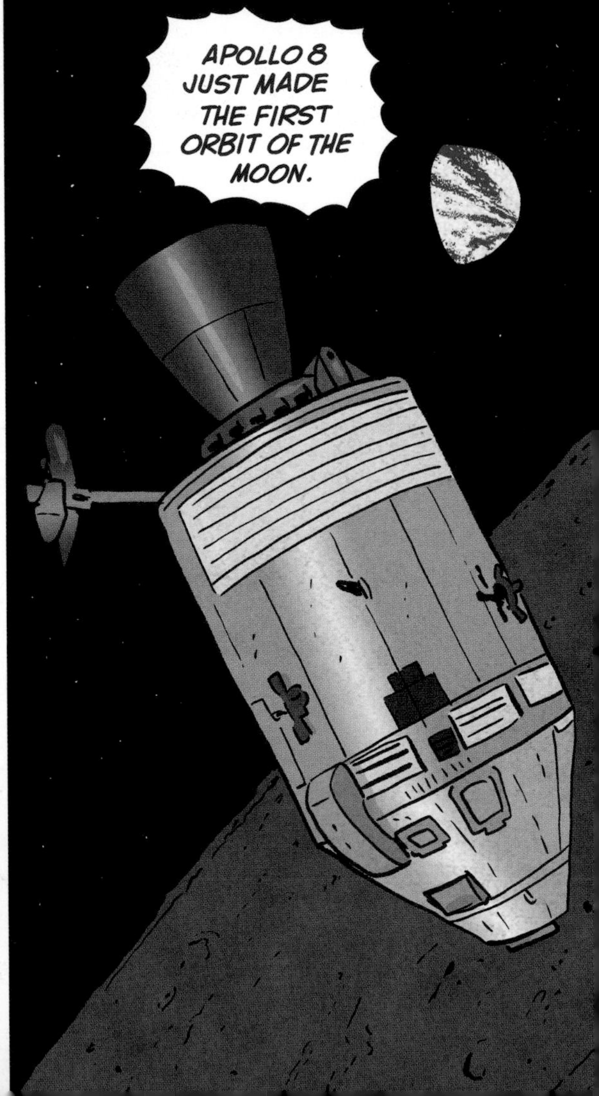
APOLLO 8 JUST MADE THE FIRST ORBIT OF THE MOON.

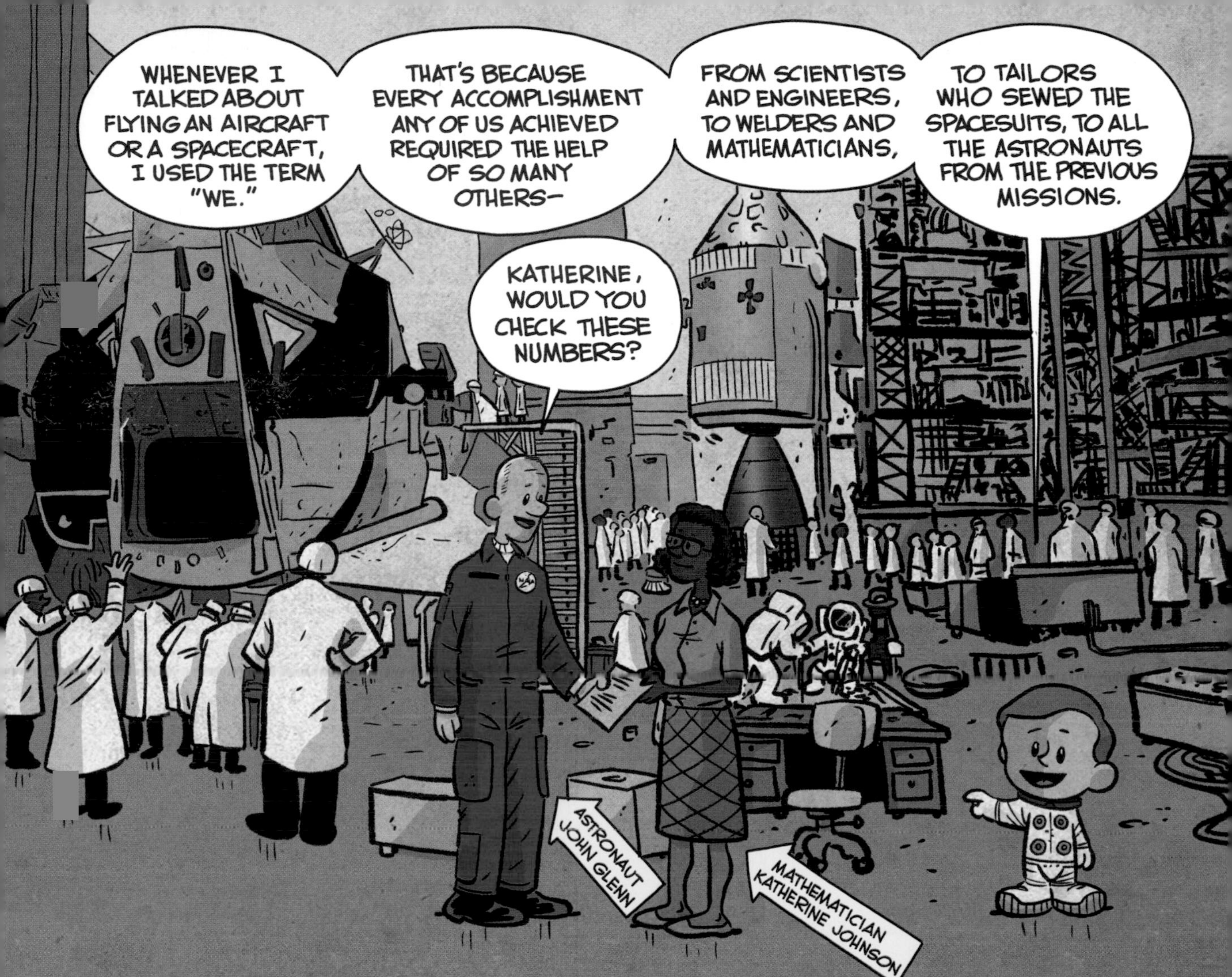
WHENEVER I TALKED ABOUT FLYING AN AIRCRAFT OR A SPACECRAFT, I USED THE TERM "WE."
THAT'S BECAUSE EVERY ACCOMPLISHMENT ANY OF US ACHIEVED REQUIRED THE HELP OF SO MANY OTHERS–
FROM SCIENTISTS AND ENGINEERS, TO WELDERS AND MATHEMATICIANS,
TO TAILORS WHO SEWED THE SPACESUITS, TO ALL THE ASTRONAUTS FROM THE PREVIOUS MISSIONS.
KATHERINE, WOULD YOU CHECK THESE NUMBERS?
ASTRONAUT JOHN GLENN
MATHEMATICIAN KATHERINE JOHNSON

When Apollo 11 was finally ready, I said to the flight director . . . "Please tell everyone who worked on this that this is their launch.

"Tell them they'll be riding with us all the way."

All that was left now was to proceed with the steps in the plan.

STEP 1: The giant Saturn V rocket had three stages. When each stage burned its fuel, the next stage would take over, giving us enough lift to get us out of Earth's gravity and into the moon's orbit.

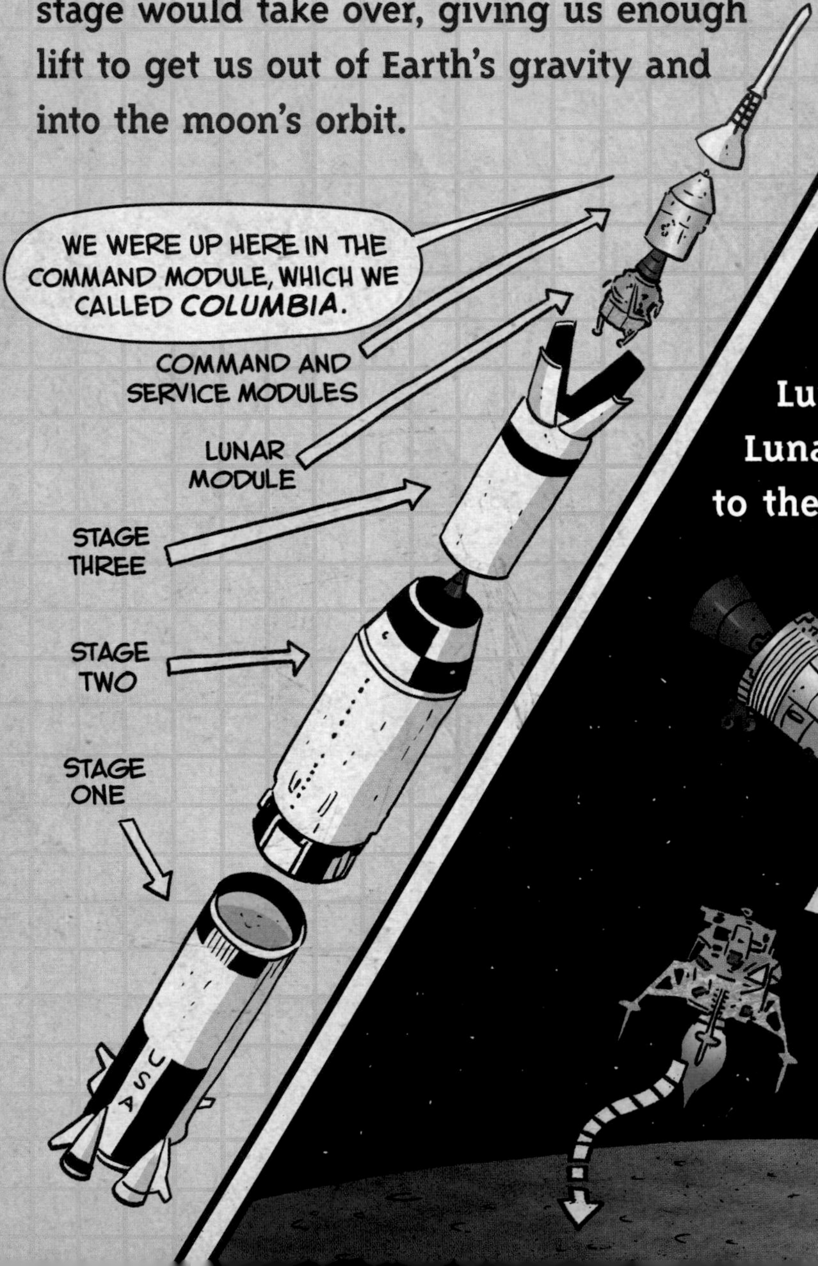
WE WERE UP HERE IN THE COMMAND MODULE, WHICH WE CALLED COLUMBIA.
COMMAND AND SERVICE MODULES
LUNAR MODULE
STAGE THREE
STAGE TWO
STAGE ONE
USA

STEP 2: When we reached the moon, the Command Module would park, circling the moon and staying in orbit.

We would move to the Lunar Module, and then the Lunar Module would go down to the surface.

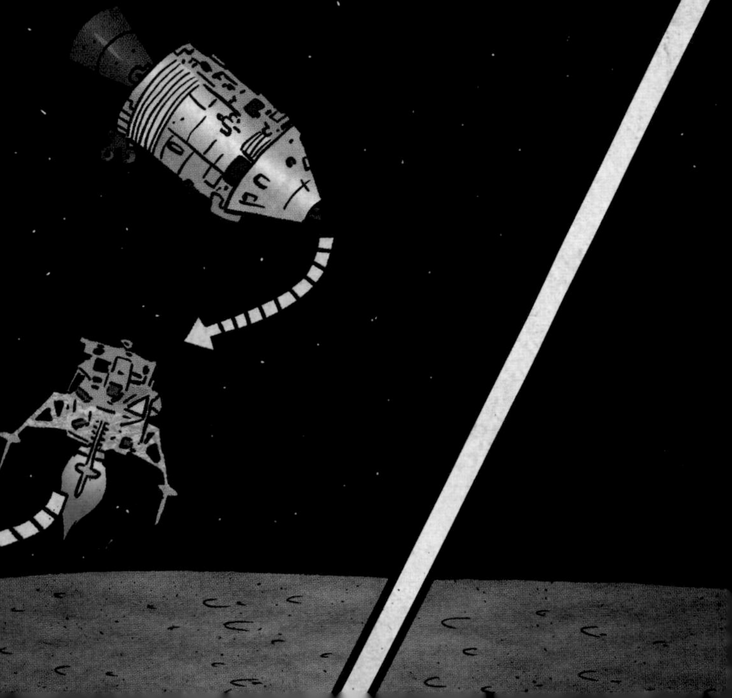

STEP 3: When we were ready to leave, the Lunar Module would lift off from the moon.

It would have to perfectly dock with the Command Module.

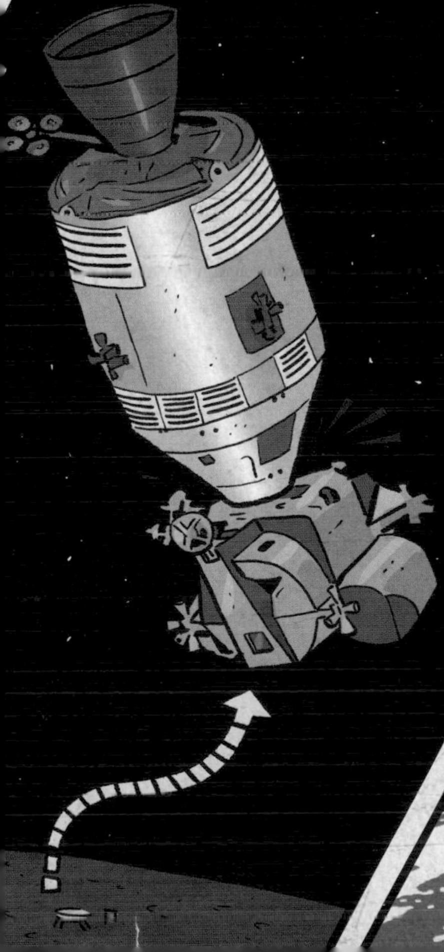

STEP 4:

Then we would climb back into the Command Module, fire the rocket on the Service Module, and come back to Earth.

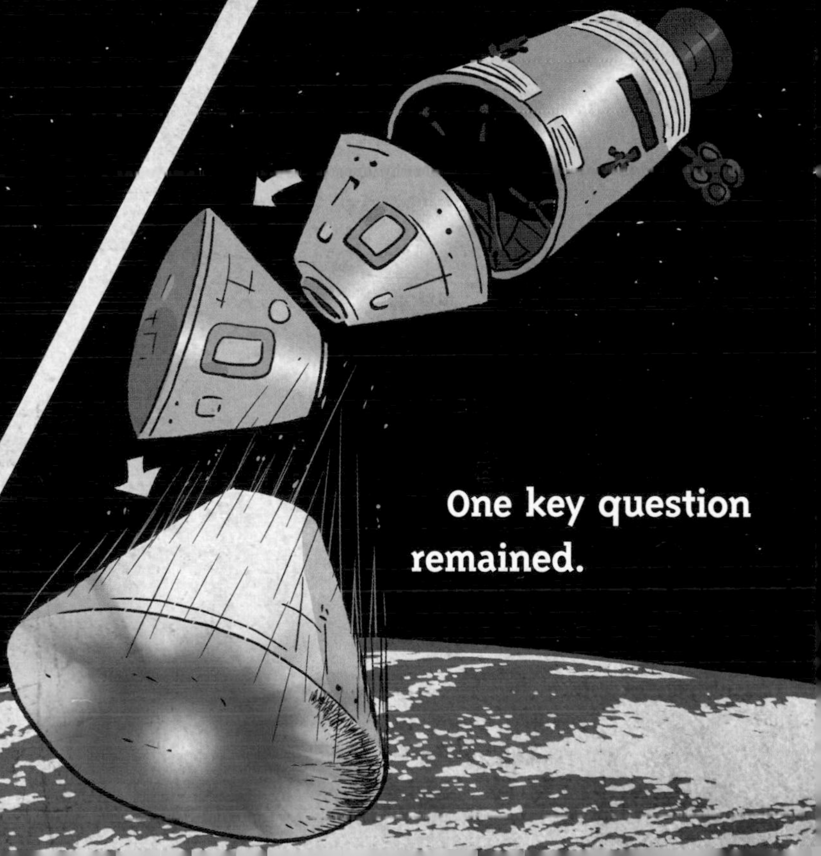

One key question remained.

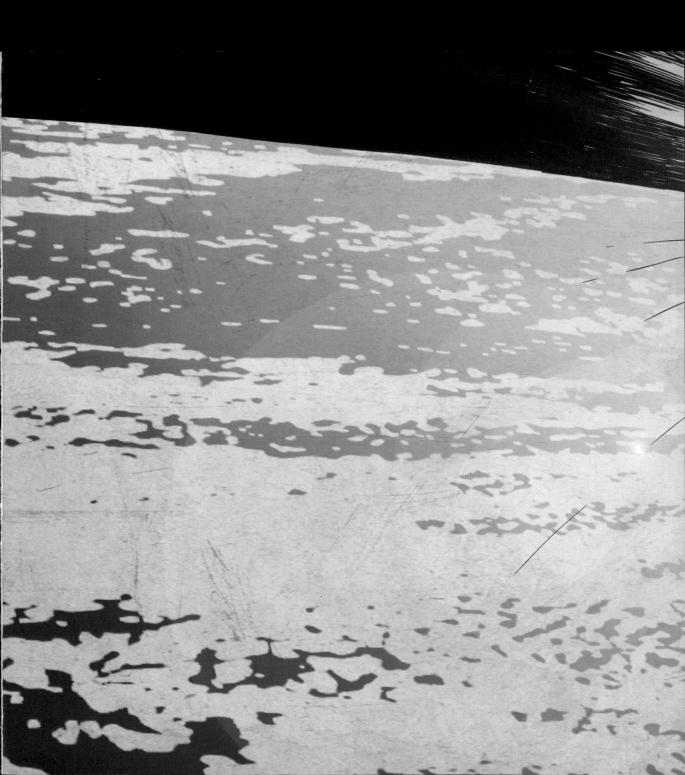

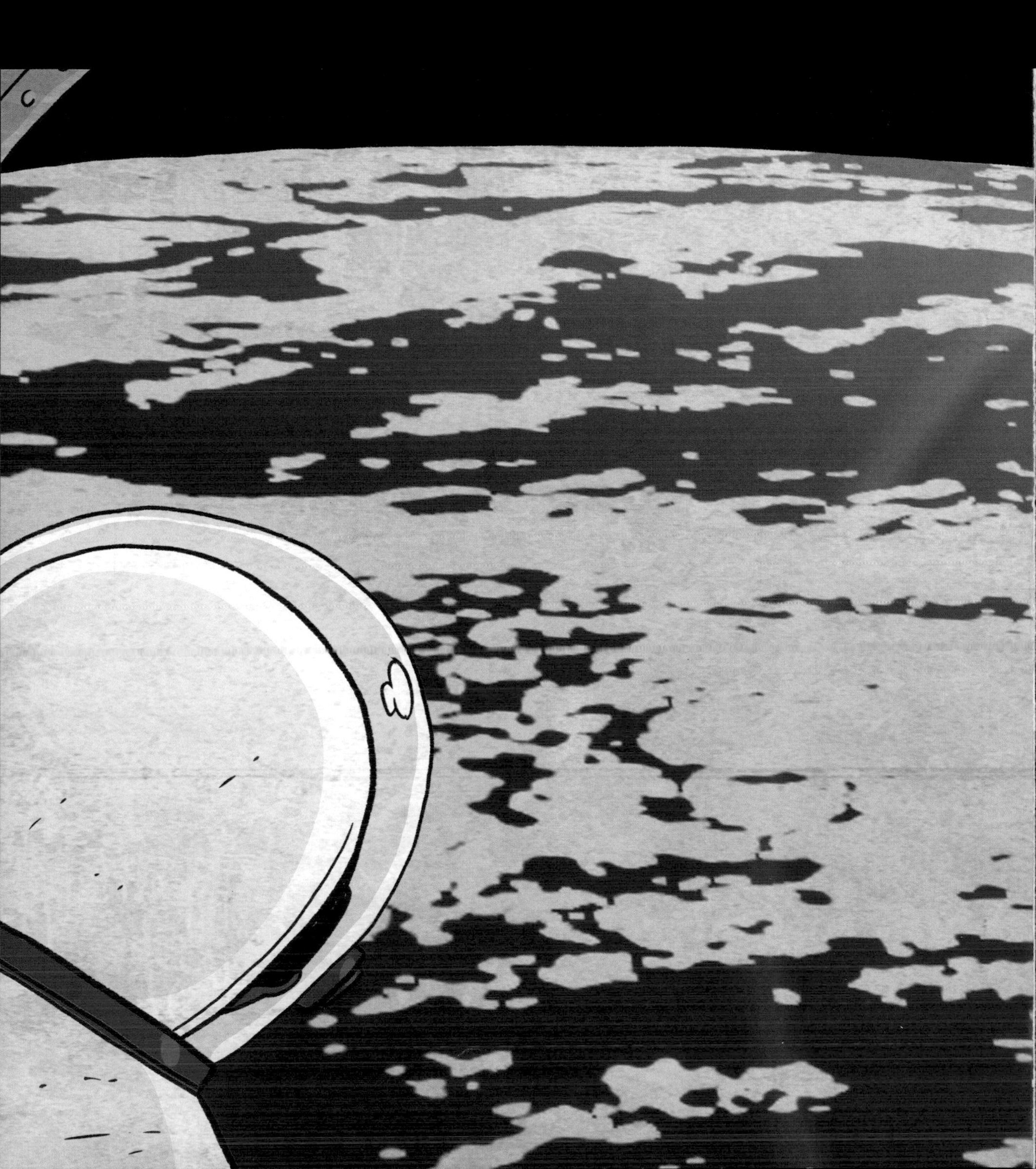

Would it work?

On July 16, 1969, at Florida's Cape Kennedy, almost one million people were there to watch.

There were three of us on board.

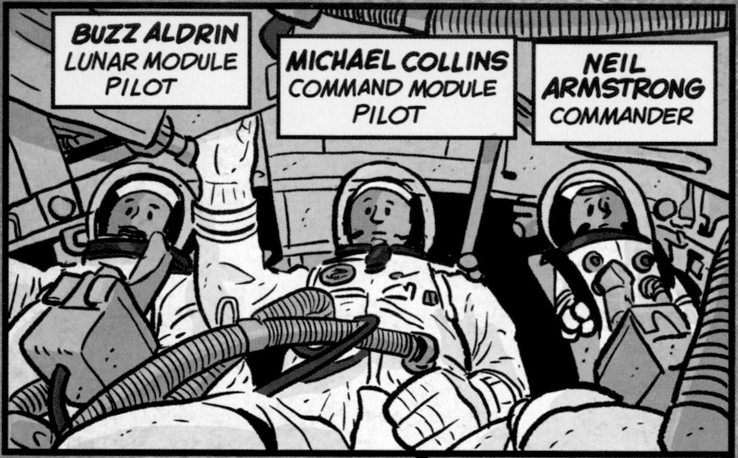
BUZZ ALDRIN
LUNAR MODULE PILOT
MICHAEL COLLINS
COMMAND MODULE PILOT
NEIL ARMSTRONG
COMMANDER

On Launchpad 39A, after a 417-step checklist to make sure everything was perfect, the countdown began. . .

12, 11, 10, 9. . . ignition sequence start. . .

4, 3, 2, 1, 0. . .

All engines running.

Liftoff!

We have a liftoff!

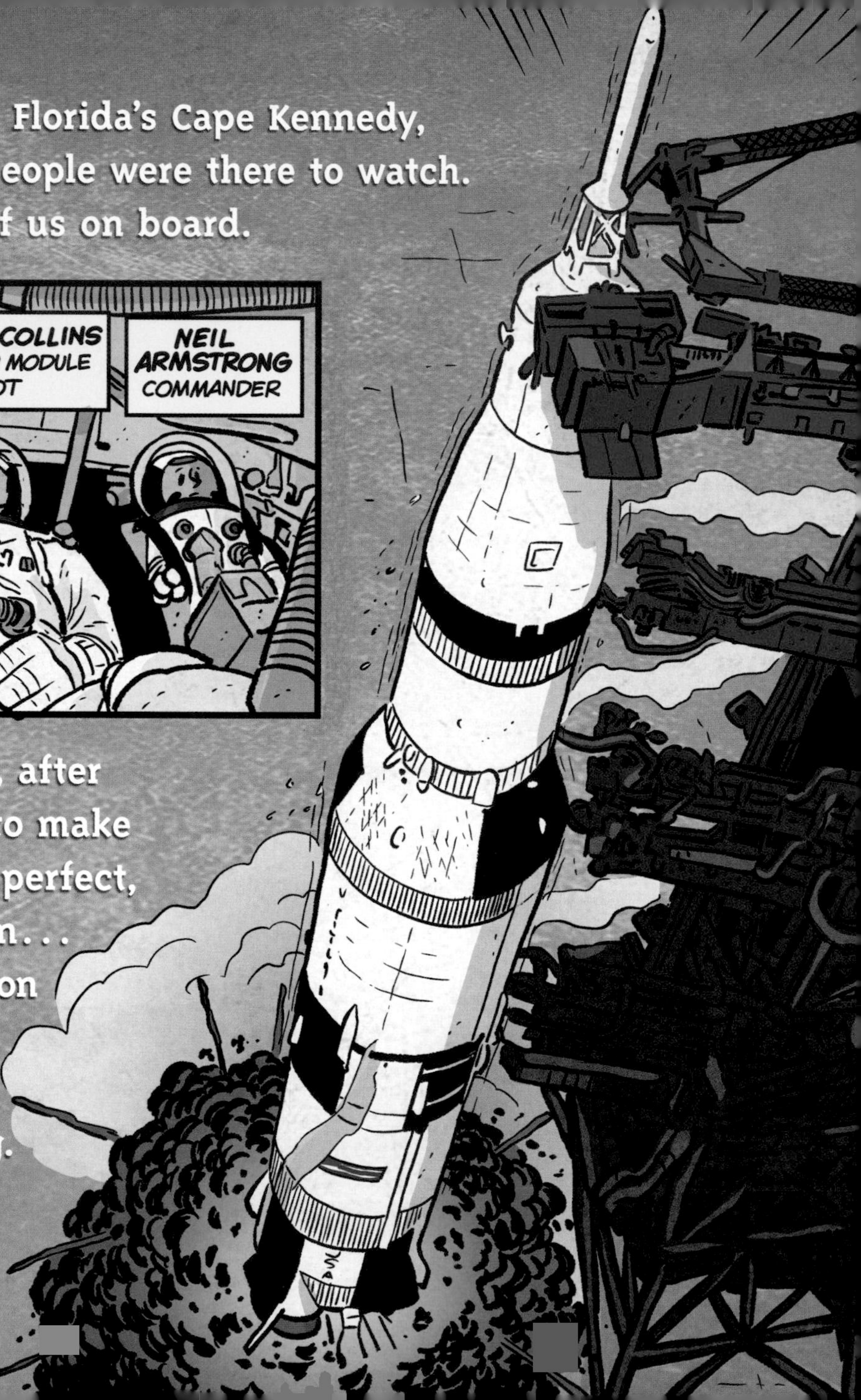

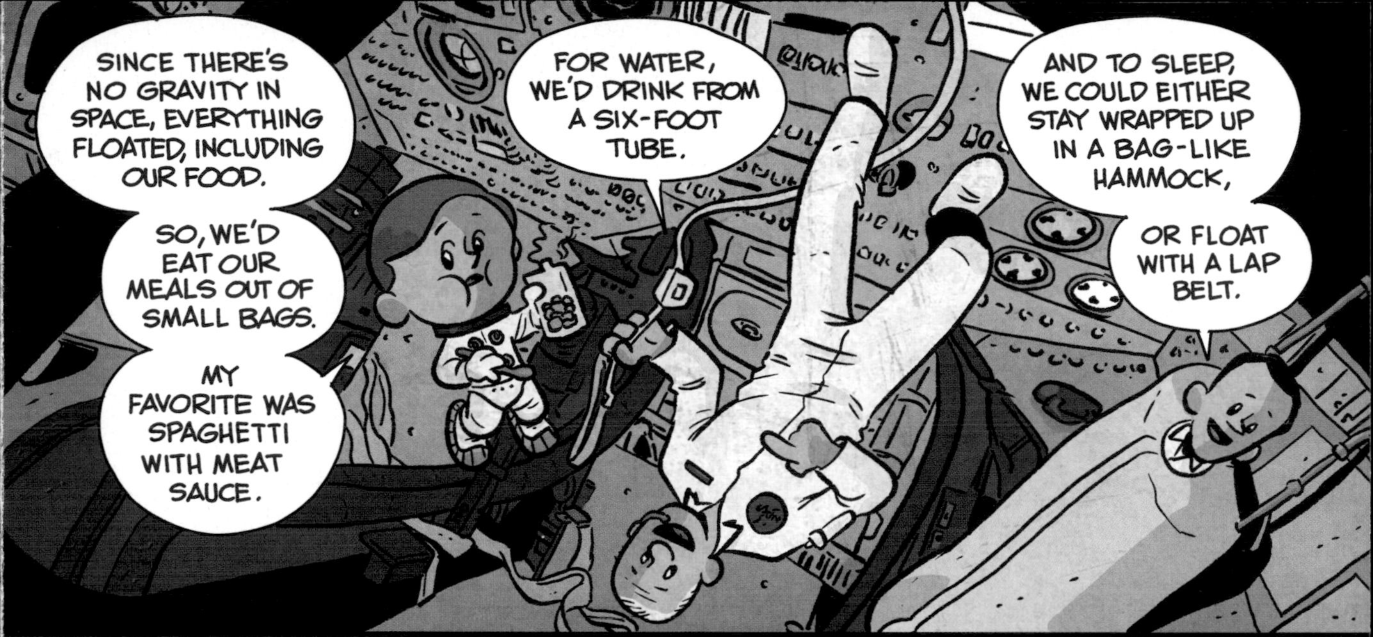
SINCE THERE'S NO GRAVITY IN SPACE, EVERYTHING FLOATED, INCLUDING OUR FOOD.
SO, WE'D EAT OUR MEALS OUT OF SMALL BAGS.
MY FAVORITE WAS SPAGHETTI WITH MEAT SAUCE.
FOR WATER, WE'D DRINK FROM A SIX-FOOT TUBE.
AND TO SLEEP, WE COULD EITHER STAY WRAPPED UP IN A BAG-LIKE HAMMOCK,
OR FLOAT WITH A LAP BELT.

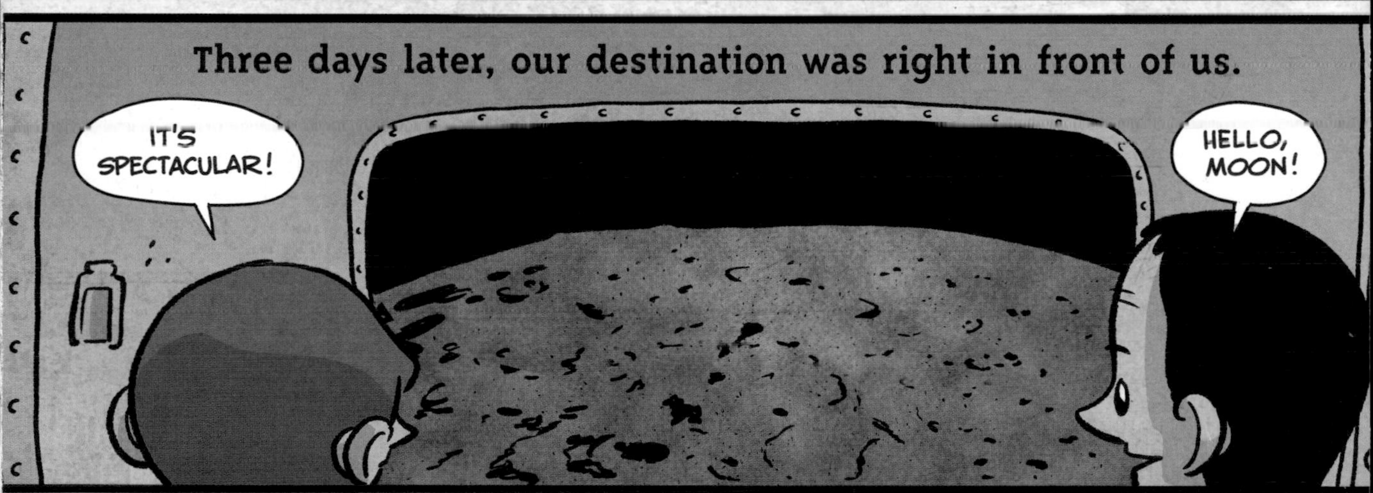
Three days later, our destination was right in front of us.
IT'S SPECTACULAR!
HELLO, MOON!

Remember our plan?

We were still following it, step by step.

Buzz and I got into Eagle.

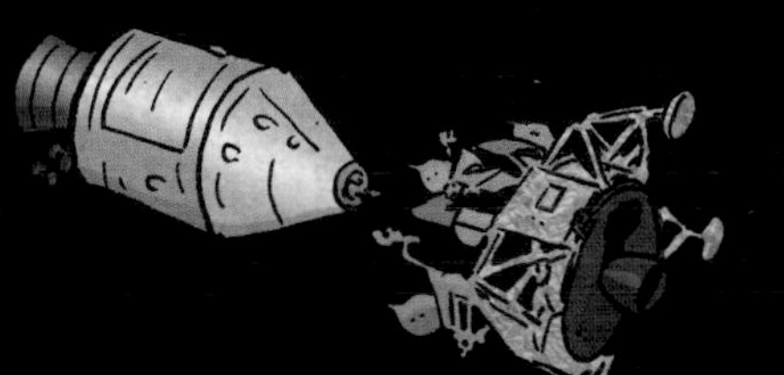

STEP 2: LUNAR MODULE **(EAGLE)** HEADS TO SURFACE ✓

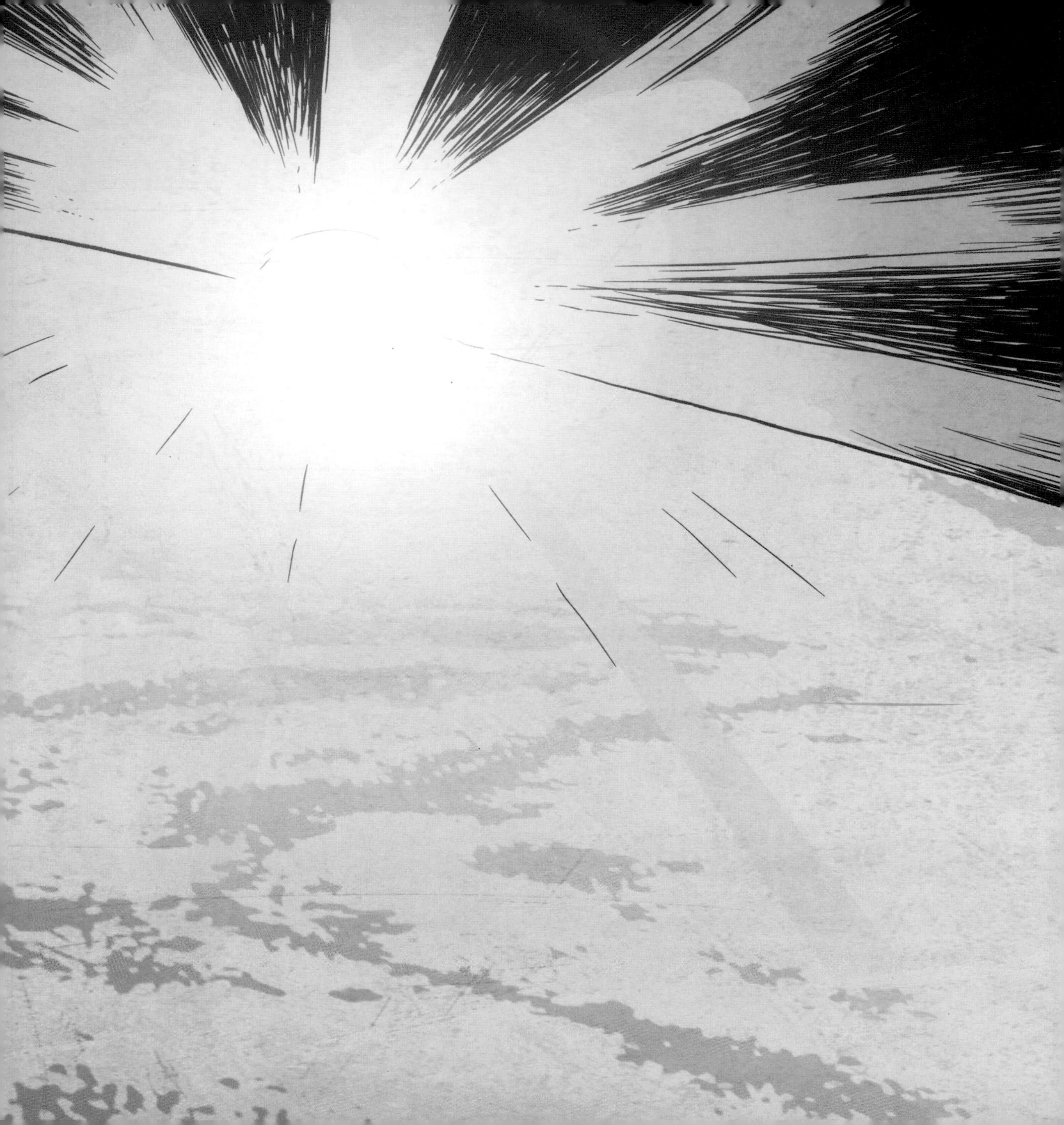

There's nothing on Earth quite like it.

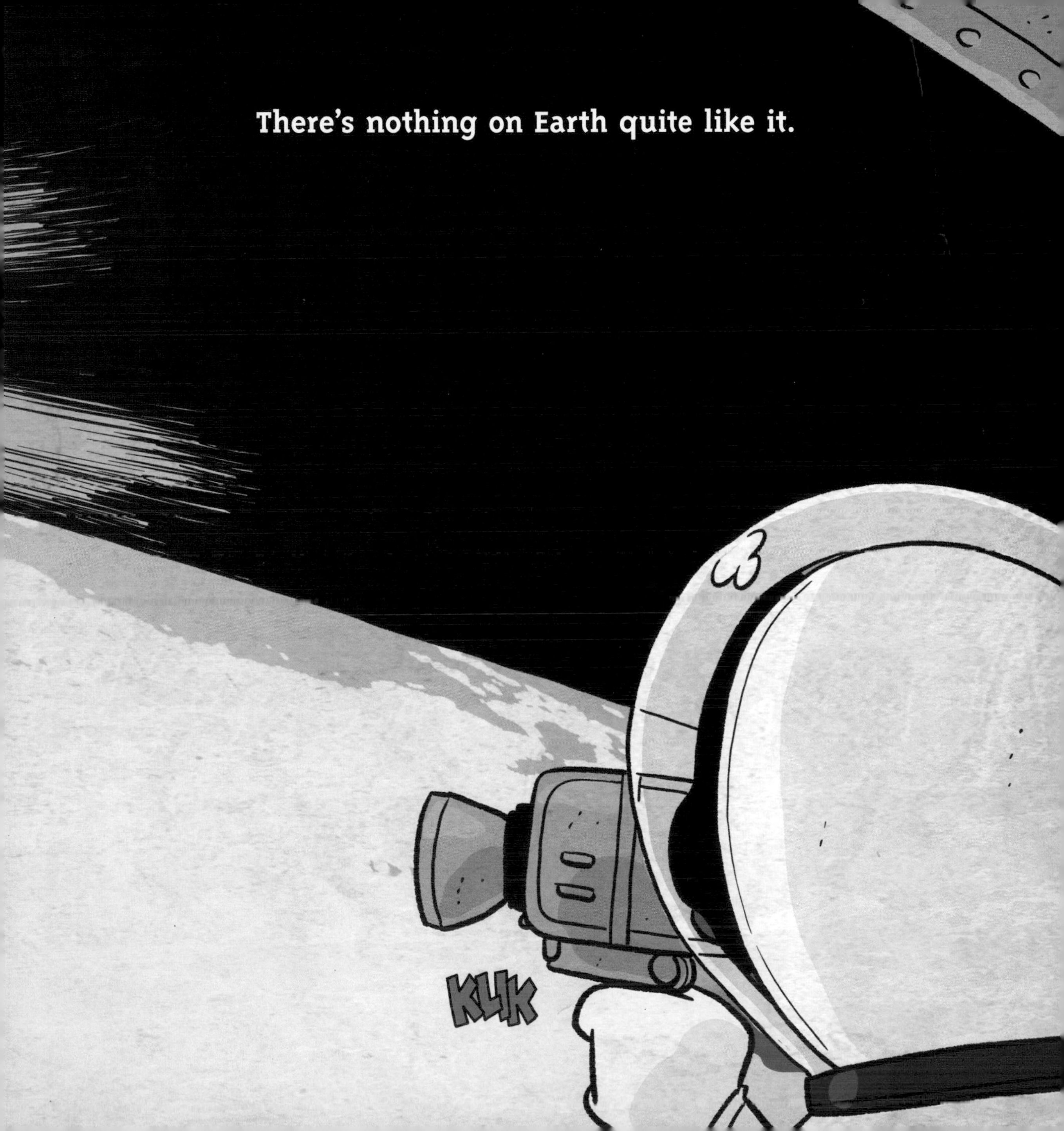
KLIK

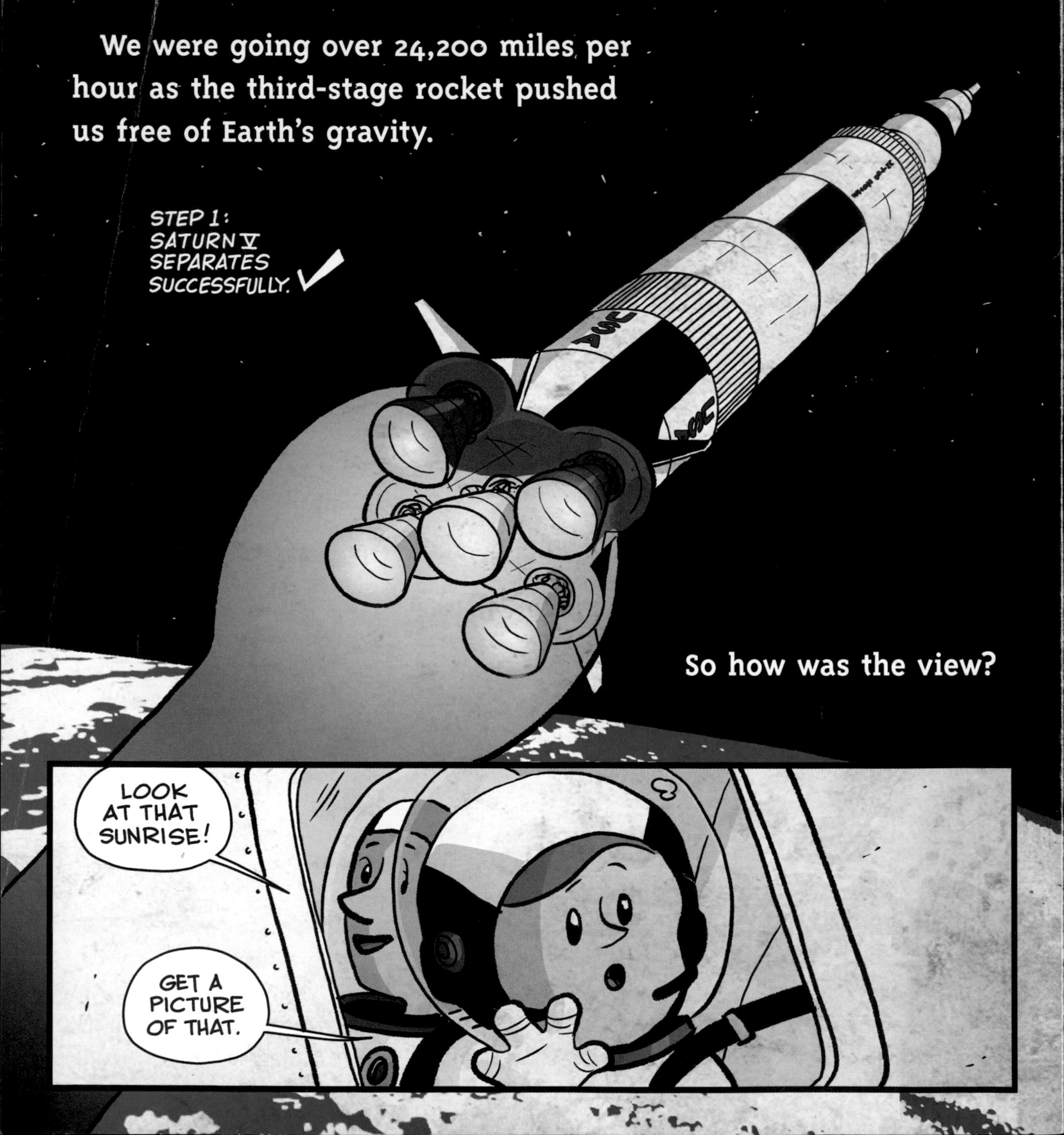
We were going over 24,200 miles per hour as the third-stage rocket pushed us free of Earth's gravity.
STEP 1: SATURN V SEPARATES SUCCESSFULLY. ✓
USA
So how was the view?
LOOK AT THAT SUNRISE!
GET A PICTURE OF THAT.

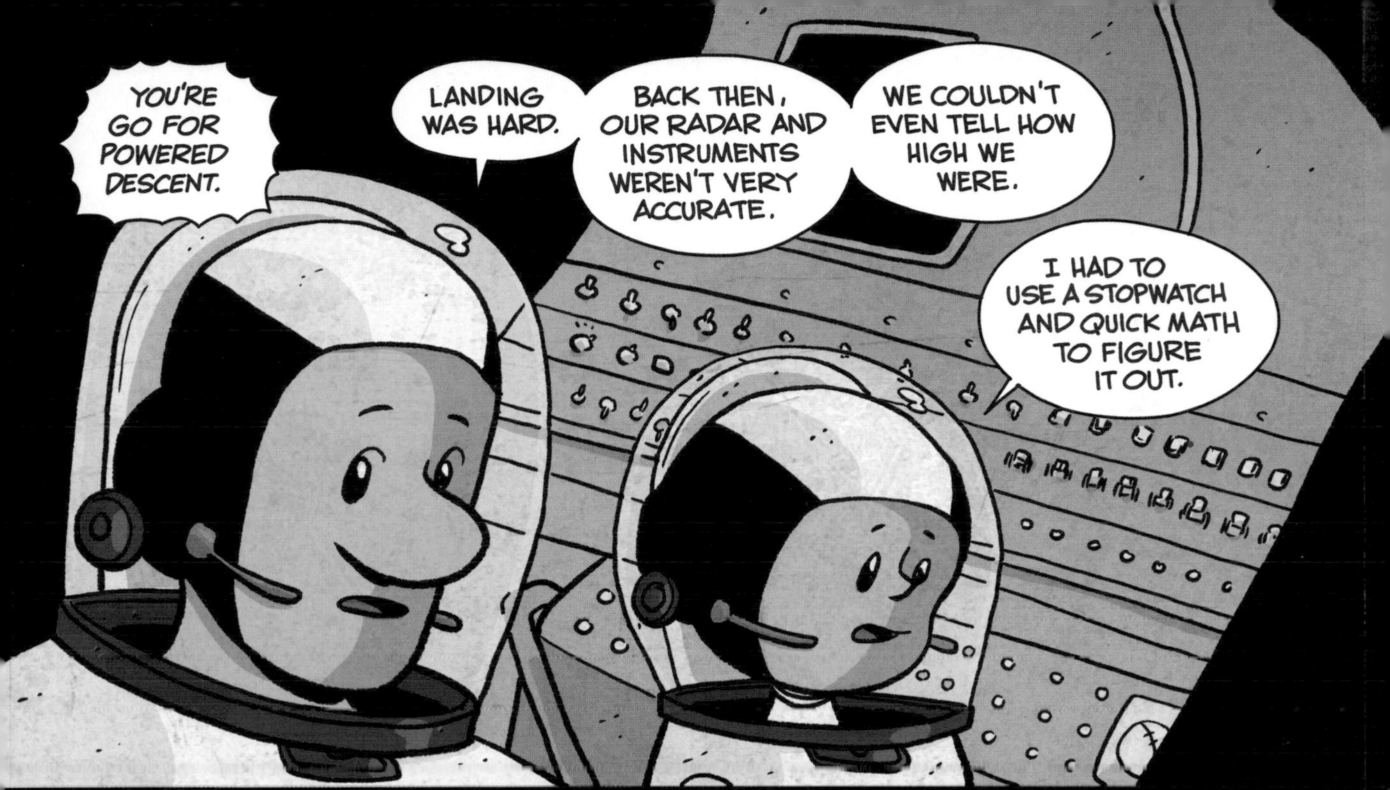
YOU'RE GO FOR POWERED DESCENT.
LANDING WAS HARD.
BACK THEN, OUR RADAR AND INSTRUMENTS WEREN'T VERY ACCURATE.
WE COULDN'T EVEN TELL HOW HIGH WE WERE.
I HAD TO USE A STOPWATCH AND QUICK MATH TO FIGURE IT OUT.

We realized we weren't close to our landing spot.
The ground wasn't smooth.
There were rocks as big as cars.

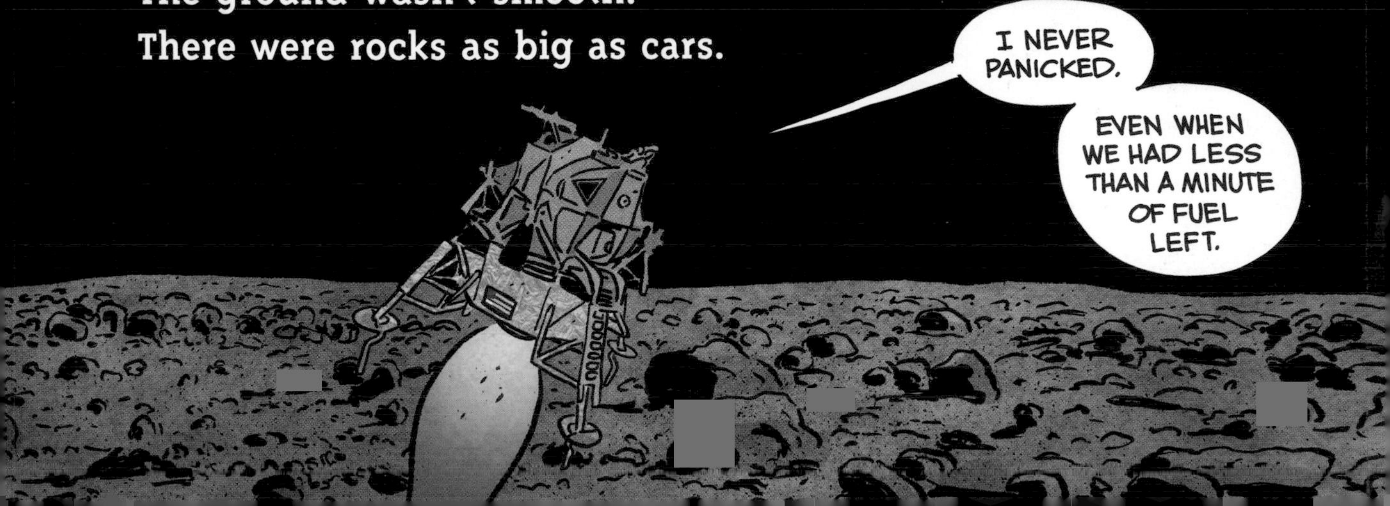
I NEVER PANICKED.
EVEN WHEN WE HAD LESS THAN A MINUTE OF FUEL LEFT.

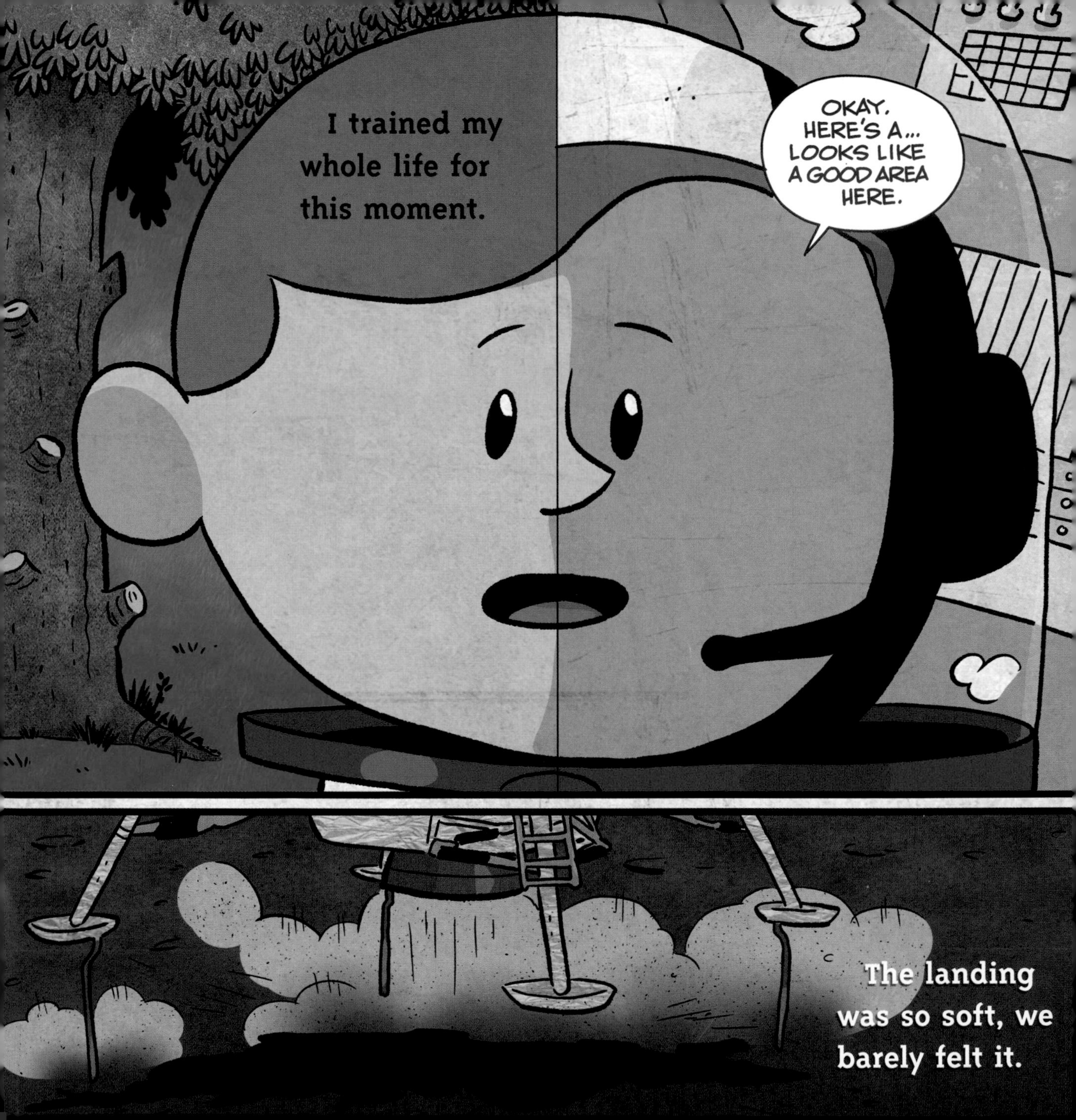
I trained my whole life for this moment.
OKAY. HERE'S A... LOOKS LIKE A GOOD AREA HERE.
The landing was so soft, we barely felt it.

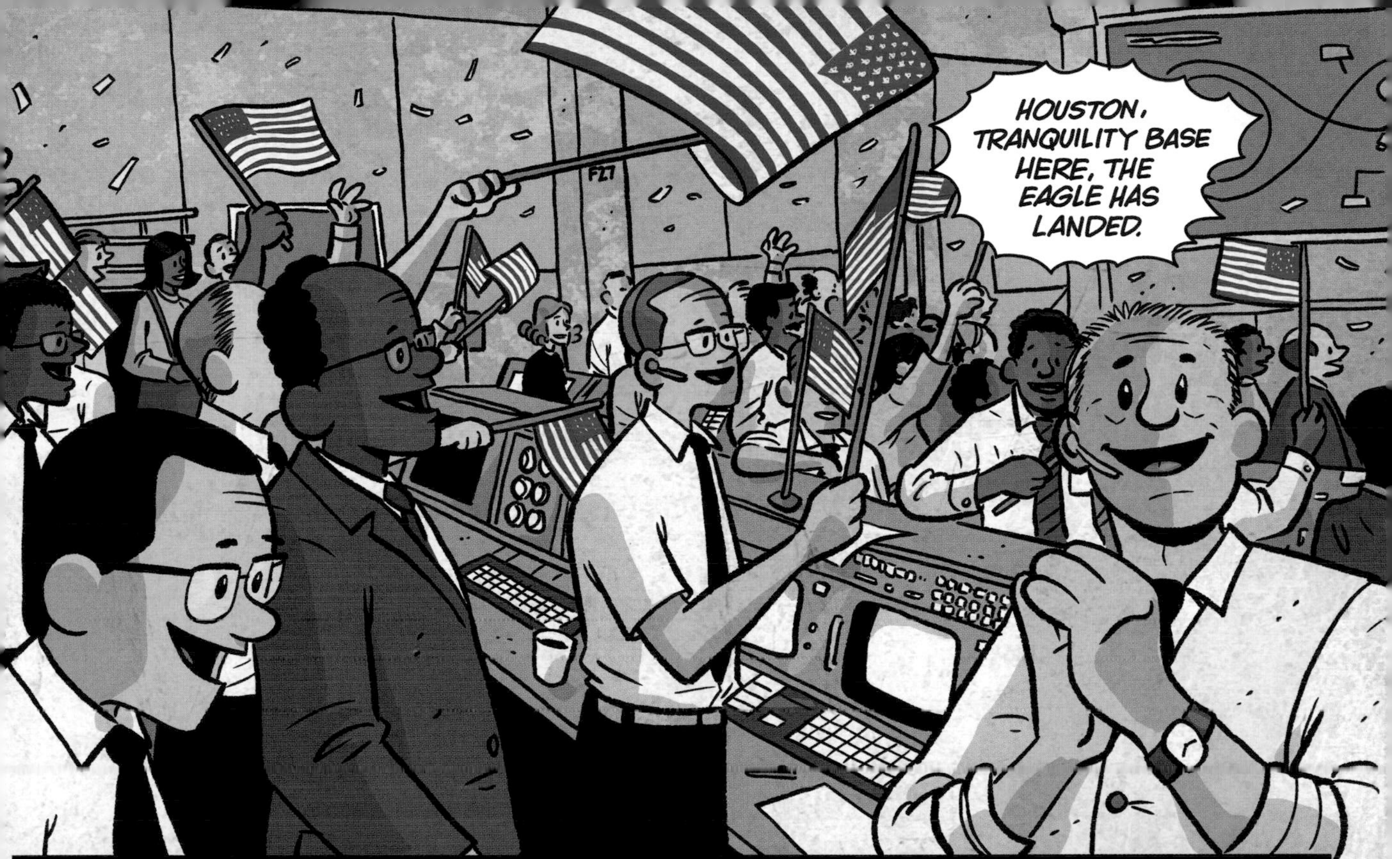
HOUSTON, TRANQUILITY BASE HERE, THE EAGLE HAS LANDED.

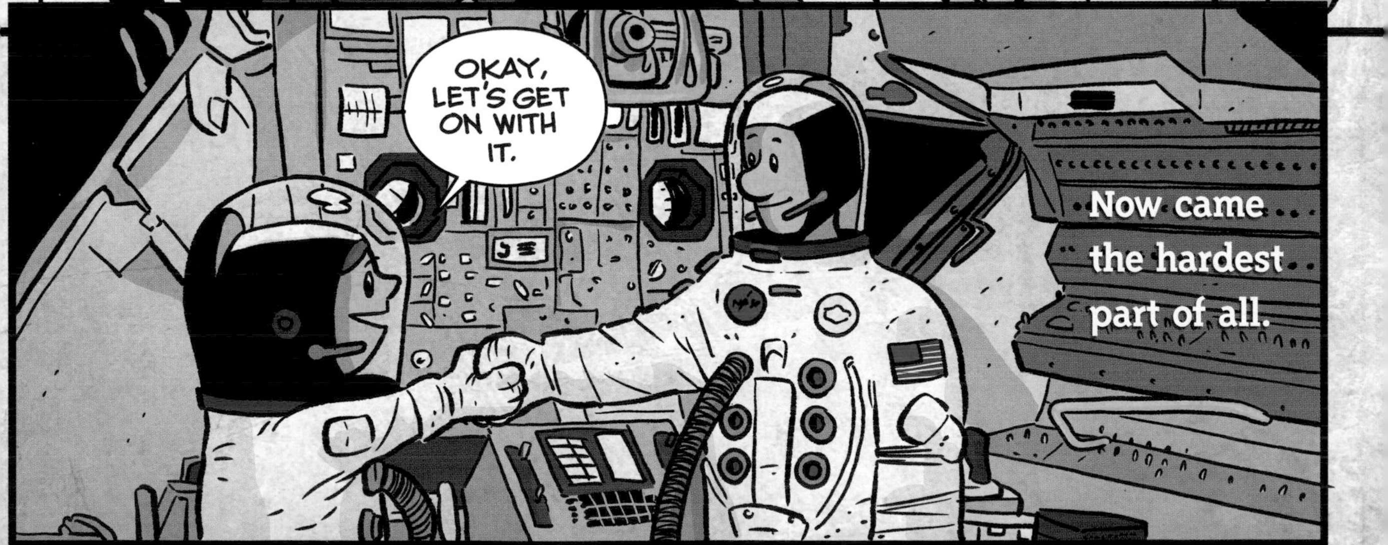
OKAY, LET'S GET ON WITH IT.
Now came the hardest part of all.

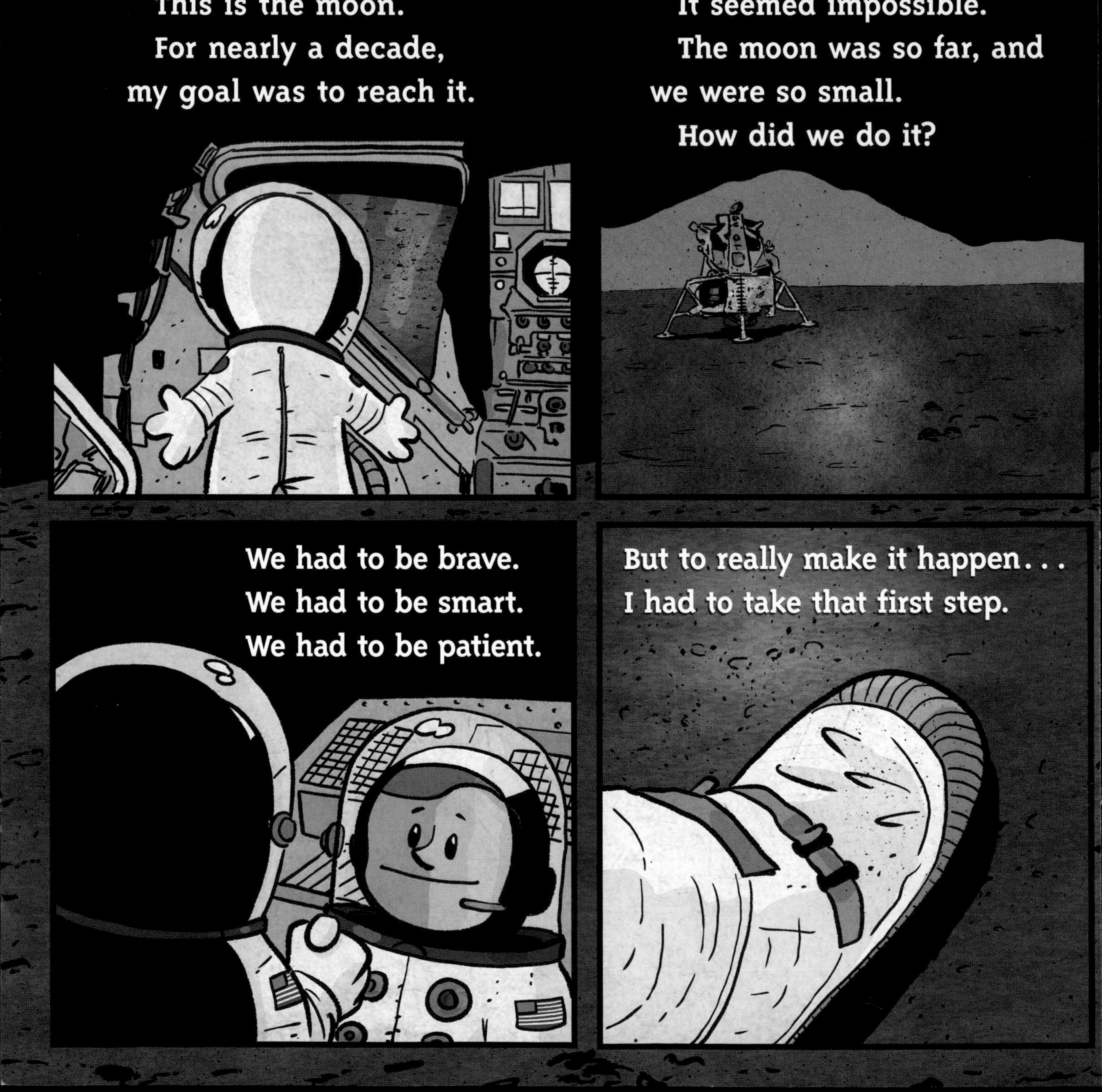
This is the moon.
For nearly a decade,
my goal was to reach it.
It seemed impossible.
The moon was so far, and
we were so small.
How did we do it?
We had to be brave.
We had to be smart.
We had to be patient.
But to really make it happen. . .
I had to take that first step.

It was 10:56 P.M. EDT—Sunday, July 20, 1969.
One-fifth of the world's population was watching on TV.

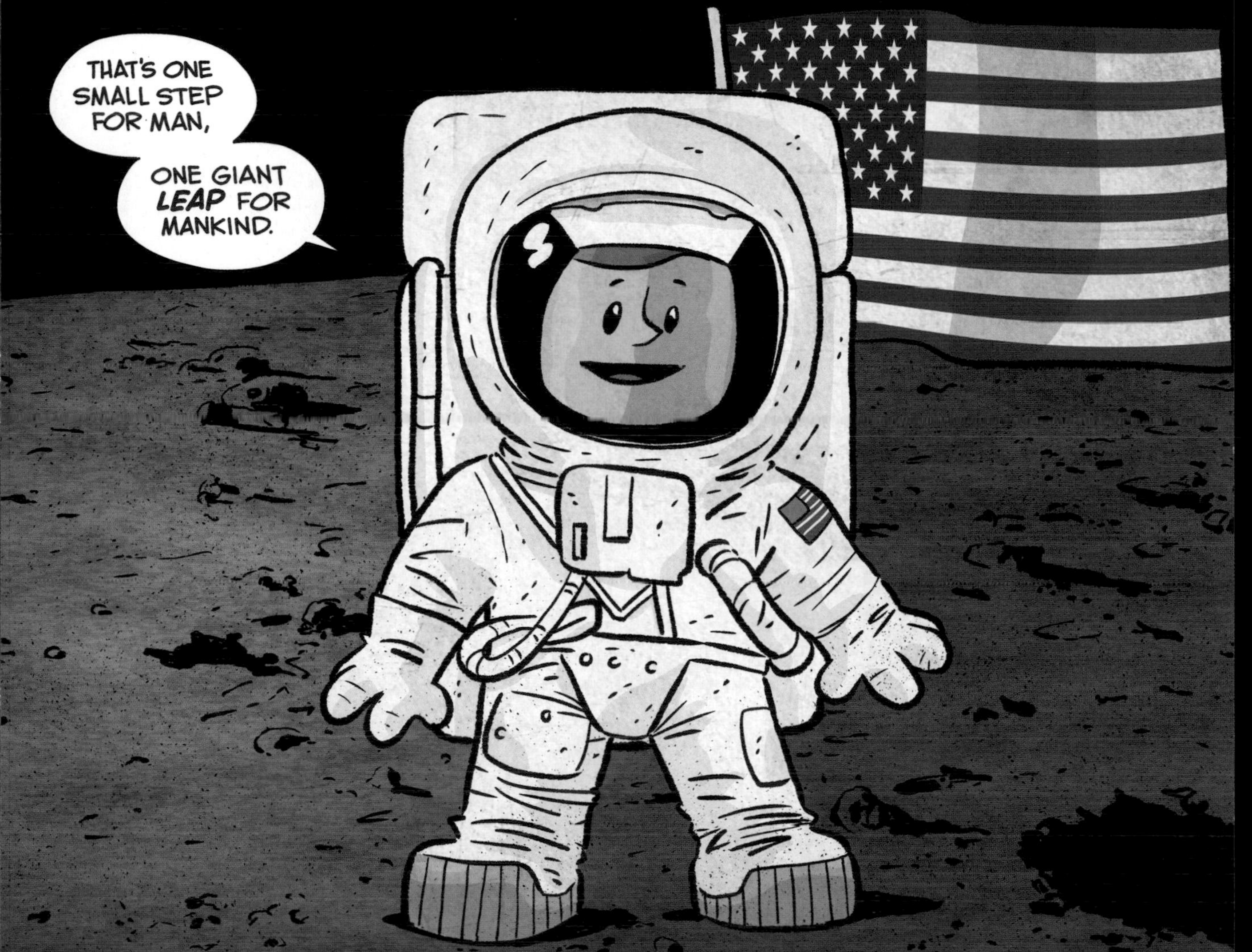
THAT'S ONE SMALL STEP FOR MAN,
ONE GIANT LEAP FOR MANKIND.

In my life, people called me a test pilot,
an astronaut, a space traveler.
But to reach the stars,
I needed to be an engineer.
Engineers search for solutions.
They solve problems.
How?
By testing and failing,
and testing and failing.

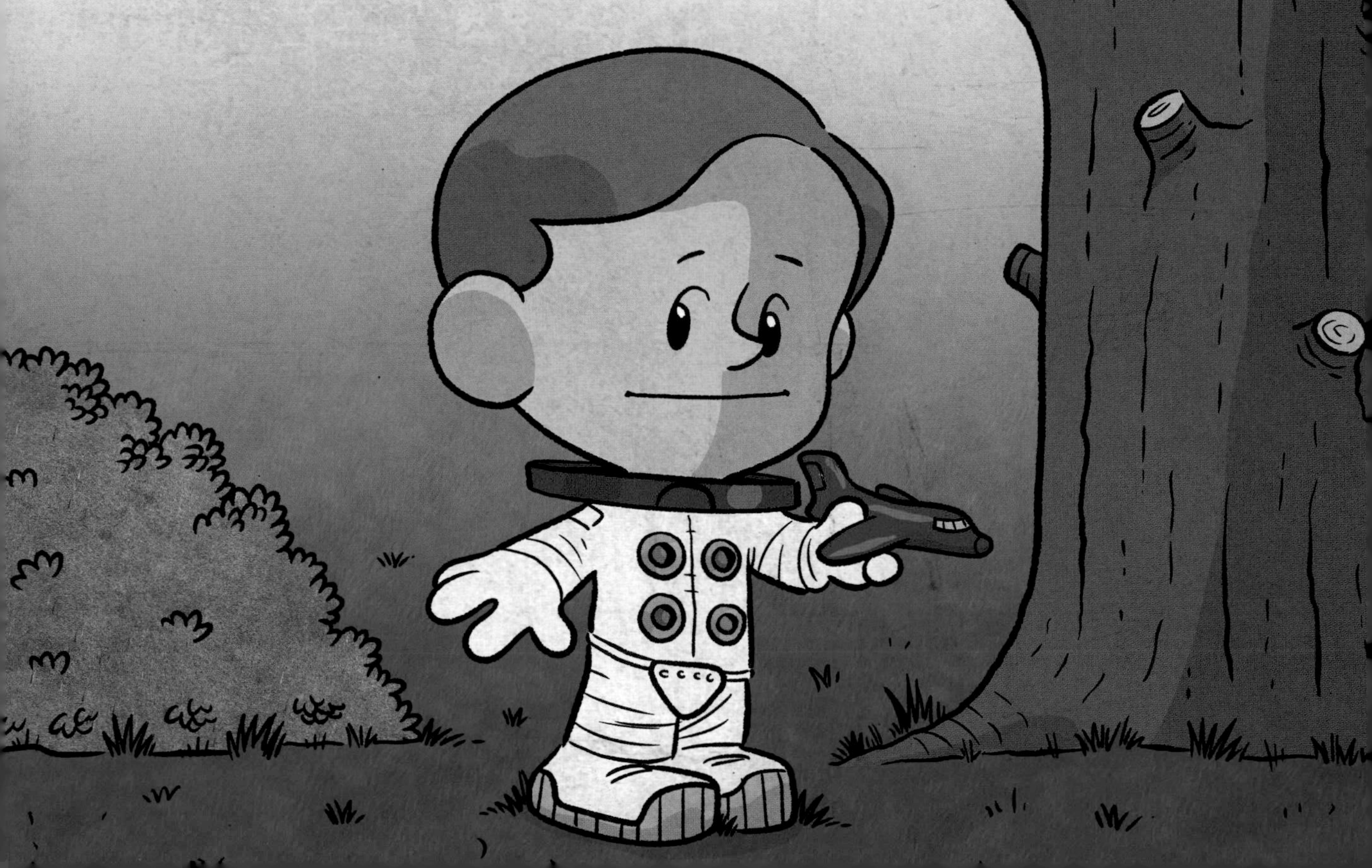

It is the key to science,
and also the key to life.
It was never just one small step that got me there.
It was the thousands that came before it.
We all have moments when we fail.
But failure is not an ending—
it's an opportunity to learn something new.
Whenever you tumble, you must get back up.
Every mistake you make teaches you a better way forward.

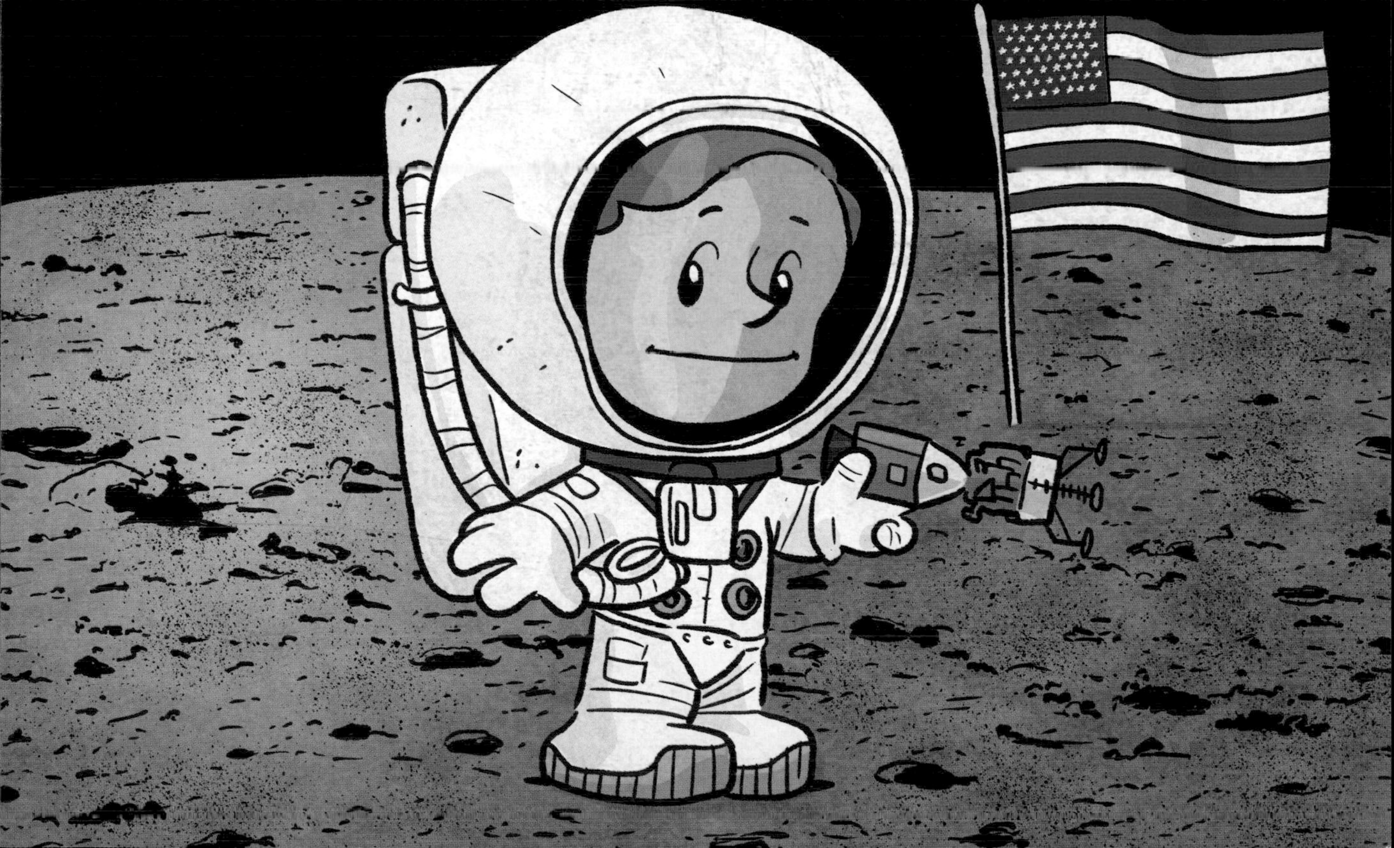

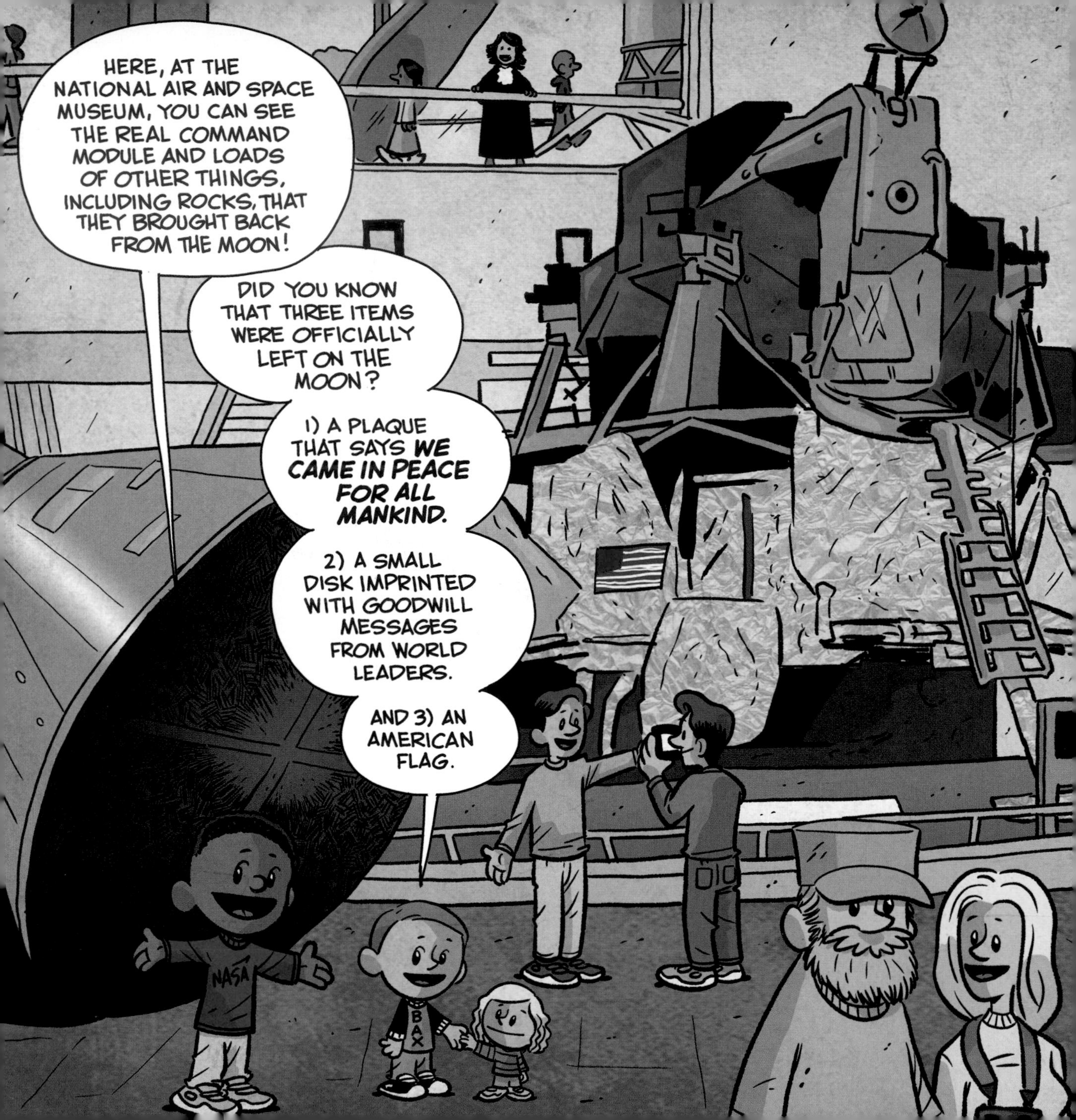
HERE, AT THE NATIONAL AIR AND SPACE MUSEUM, YOU CAN SEE THE REAL COMMAND MODULE AND LOADS OF OTHER THINGS, INCLUDING ROCKS, THAT THEY BROUGHT BACK FROM THE MOON!
DID YOU KNOW THAT THREE ITEMS WERE OFFICIALLY LEFT ON THE MOON?
1) A PLAQUE THAT SAYS **WE CAME IN PEACE FOR ALL MANKIND.**
2) A SMALL DISK IMPRINTED WITH GOODWILL MESSAGES FROM WORLD LEADERS.
AND 3) AN AMERICAN FLAG.
NASA
BAX

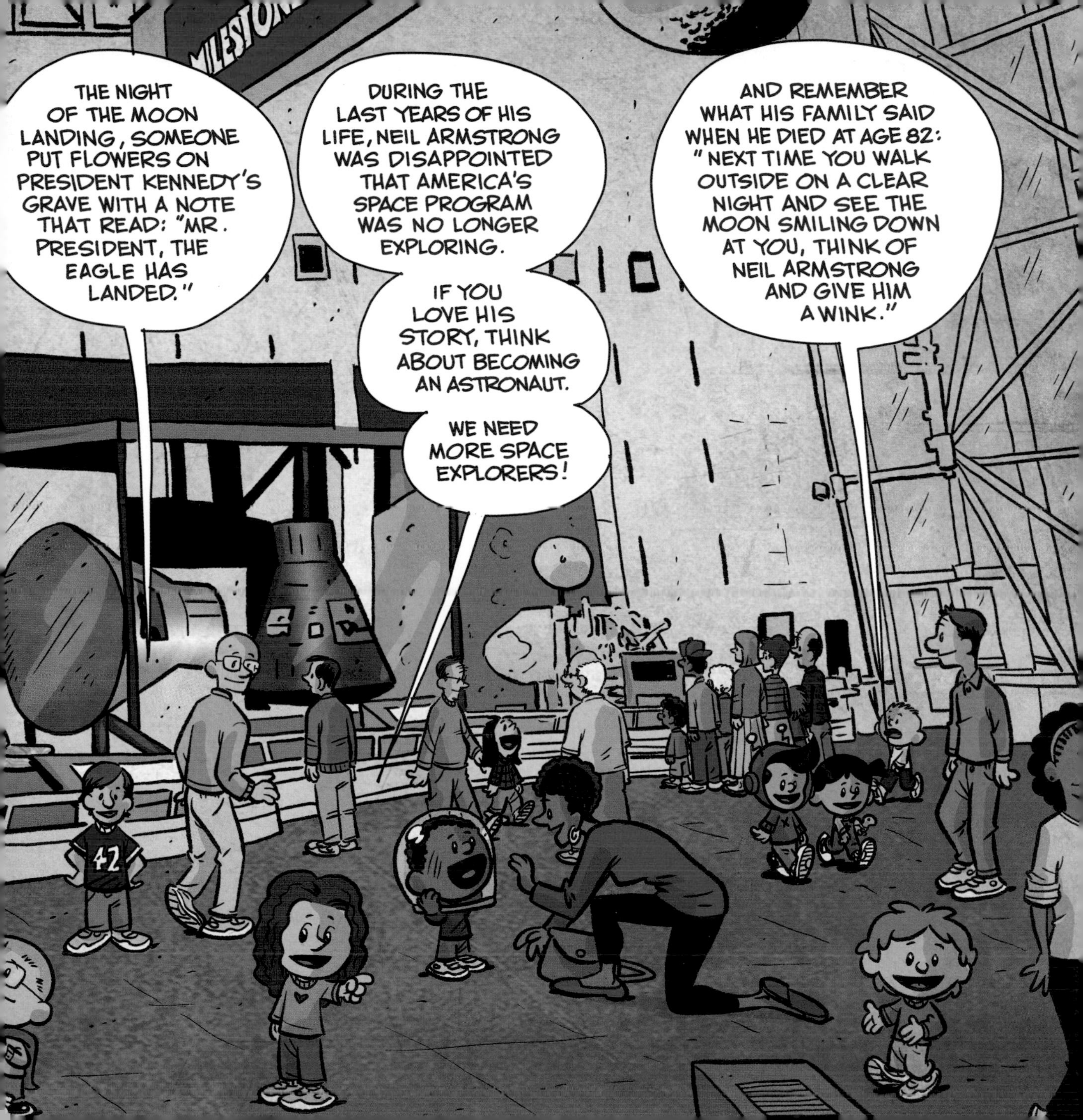
MILESTONES
THE NIGHT OF THE MOON LANDING, SOMEONE PUT FLOWERS ON PRESIDENT KENNEDY'S GRAVE WITH A NOTE THAT READ: "MR. PRESIDENT, THE EAGLE HAS LANDED."
DURING THE LAST YEARS OF HIS LIFE, NEIL ARMSTRONG WAS DISAPPOINTED THAT AMERICA'S SPACE PROGRAM WAS NO LONGER EXPLORING.
IF YOU LOVE HIS STORY, THINK ABOUT BECOMING AN ASTRONAUT.
WE NEED MORE SPACE EXPLORERS!
AND REMEMBER WHAT HIS FAMILY SAID WHEN HE DIED AT AGE 82: "NEXT TIME YOU WALK OUTSIDE ON A CLEAR NIGHT AND SEE THE MOON SMILING DOWN AT YOU, THINK OF NEIL ARMSTRONG AND GIVE HIM A WINK."
42

Whatever your path is in life, explore your dreams.
Use hard work and teamwork.
Be brave and patient.
Engineer your own solutions.
It can take you all the way to the moon.

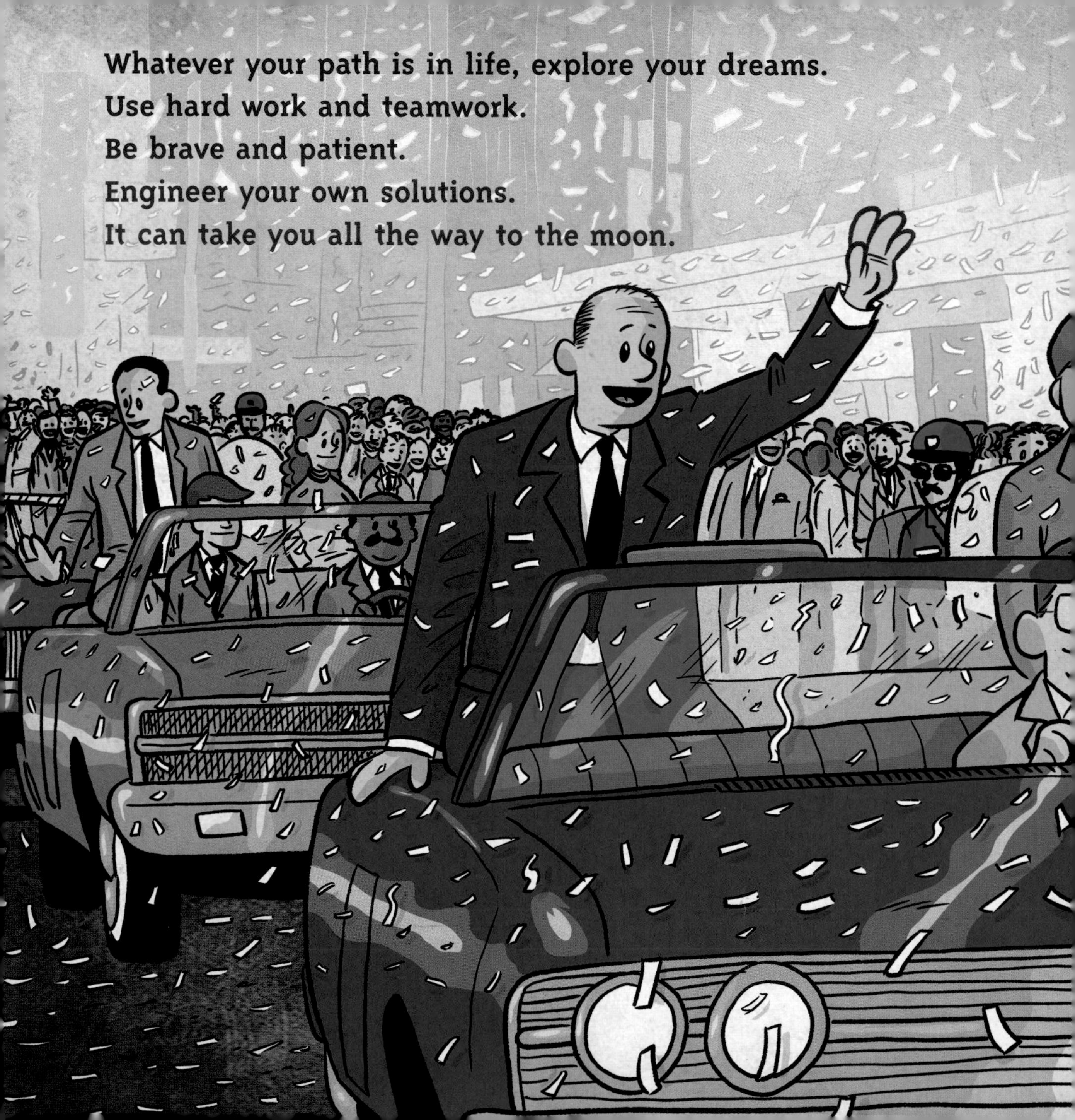

I am Neil Armstrong.
I know that every journey begins with a first step.

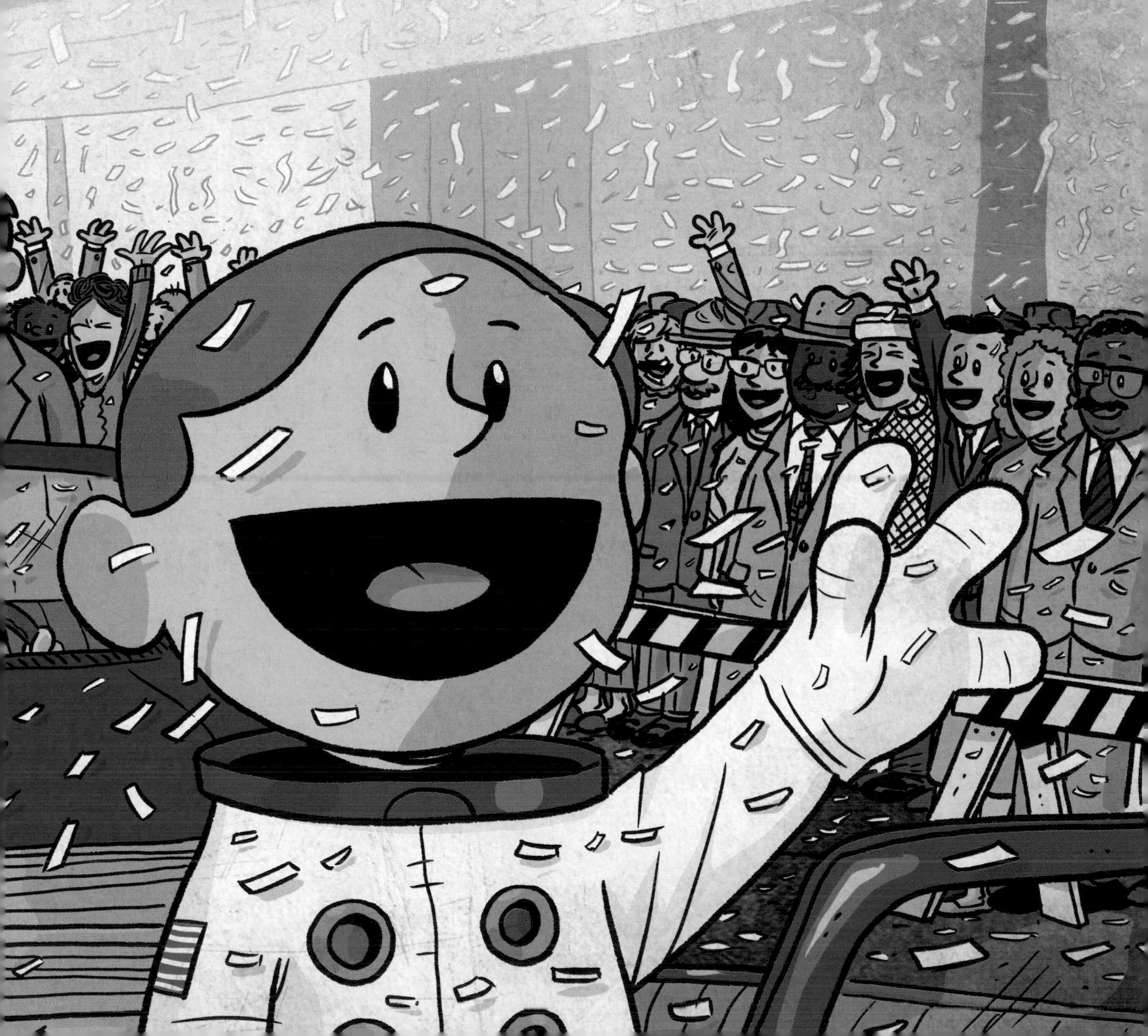

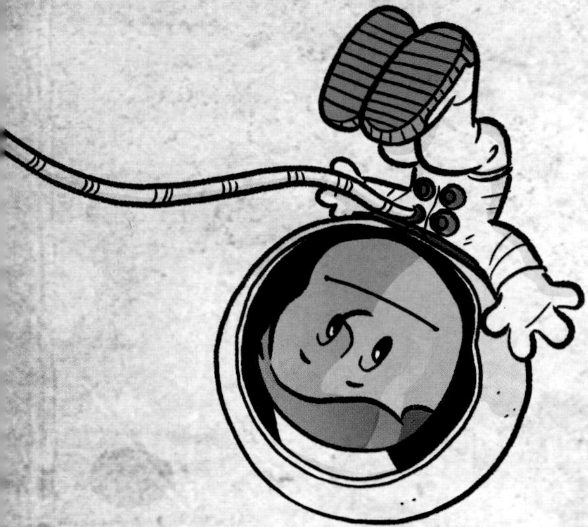

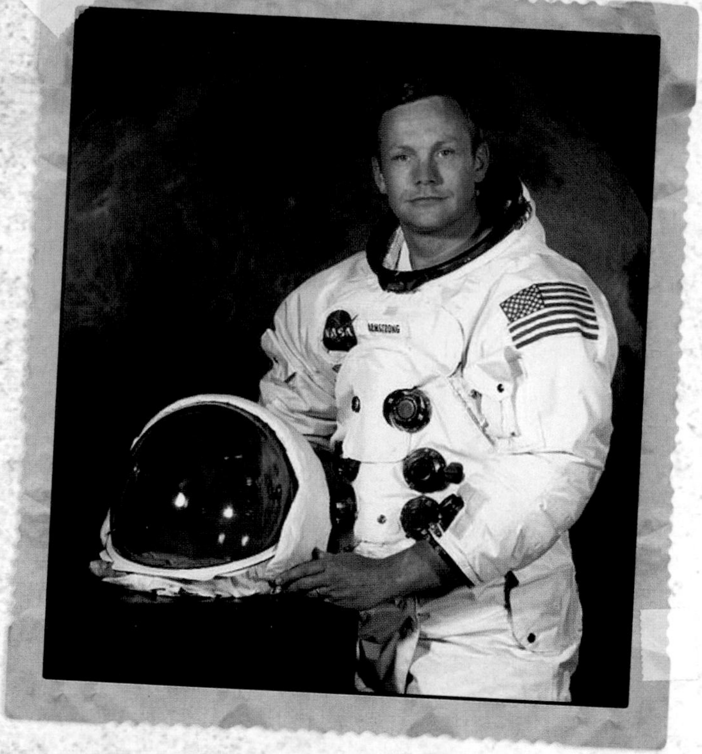

"We're going to the moon because it's in the nature of the human being to face challenges."

—Neil Armstrong

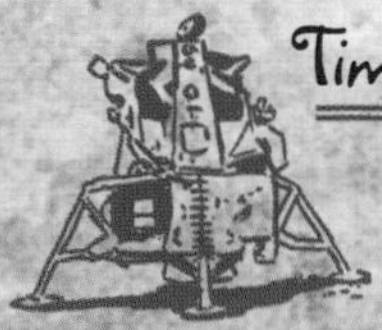

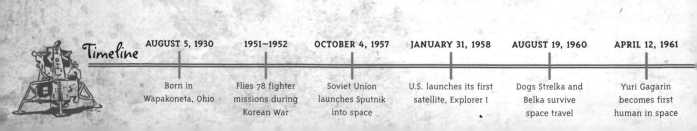

Timeline

AUGUST 5, 1930	1951–1952	OCTOBER 4, 1957	JANUARY 31, 1958	AUGUST 19, 1960	APRIL 12, 1961
Born in Wapakoneta, Ohio	Flies 78 fighter missions during Korean War	Soviet Union launches Sputnik into space	U.S. launches its first satellite, Explorer 1	Dogs Strelka and Belka survive space travel	Yuri Gagarin becomes first human in space

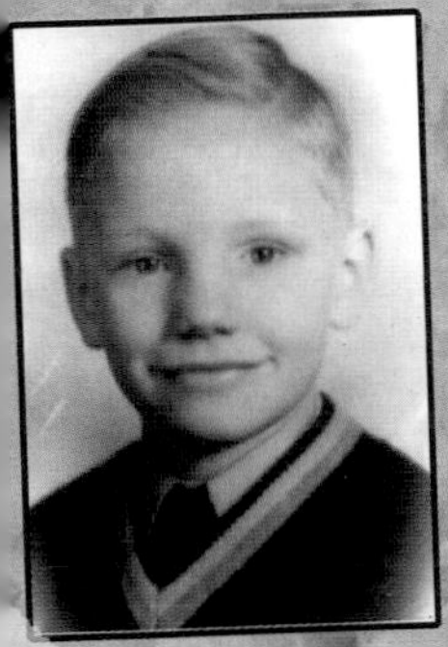

Neil as a child

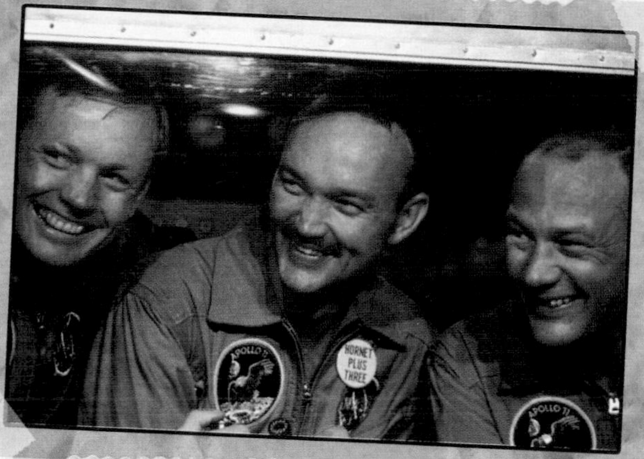
HORNET
PLUS
THREE

Neil (far left) with Michael and Buzz, 1969

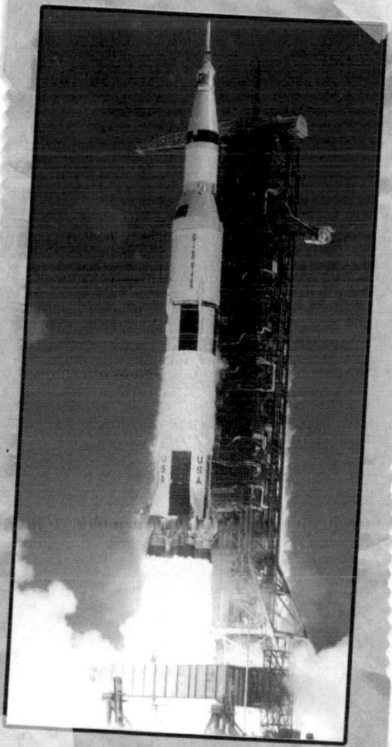

Apollo 11 launch

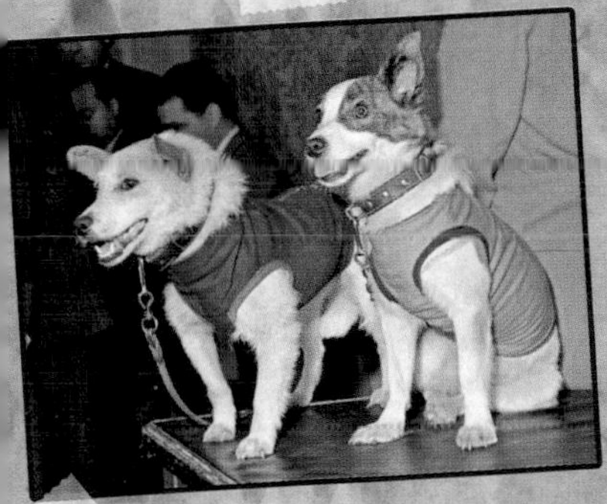

Strelka and Belka

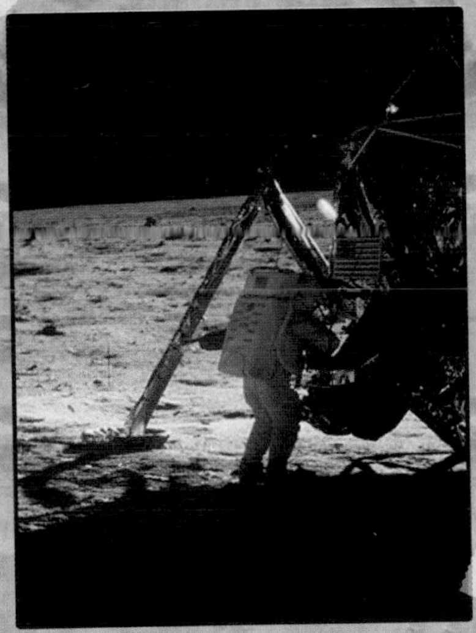

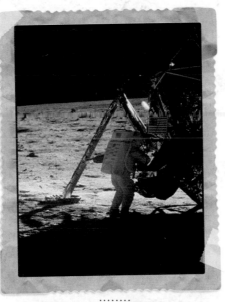

Neil standing on the surface of the moon

MAY 5, 1961	MAY 25, 1961	MARCH 16, 1966	DECEMBER 21, 1968	JULY 20, 1969	AUGUST 25, 2012
Alan Shepard becomes first American in space	President John F. Kennedy's space-race challenge	Performs first successful docking of two spacecraft (Gemini VIII mission)	Apollo 8 mission: first humans to orbit the moon	Along with Buzz Aldrin, becomes first human to land and walk on the moon	Dies during heart surgery in Cincinnati, Ohio, at age 82

For Chris Eliopoulos, my brother on these books,
and the nicest person in history.
Thank you for taking me on one of the greatest rides of my life.
—B.M.

For The Buonomo Family.
Anthony, Patty, Anna, and Lauren.
Wonderful people whom I'm lucky to call friends.
—C.E.

For historical accuracy, we used Neil Armstrong's actual dialogue whenever possible. For more of Mr. Armstrong's true voice, we recommend and acknowledge the below titles. Special thanks to dear friend and retired NASA pilot Charlie Justiz as well as the generous Andy Chaikin for their input on early drafts. Also, thanks to NASA, for being the amazing nerds that the rest of us nerds can look up to.

· ·

SOURCES

First Man: The Life of Neil A. Armstrong by James R. Hansen (Simon & Schuster, 2005)

Neil Armstrong: A Life of Flight by Jay Barbree (St. Martin's Press, 2014)

"The Neil Armstrong I Knew" by Michael Collins, *The Washington Post* (September 13, 2012)

"'You Would Love It!' A Meeting with the First Man on the Moon" by Thanassis Vembos, *Spaceflight* magazine (July 1999)

"The Forever Spacesuit" by Kevin Dupzyk, *Popular Mechanics* (November 2015)

"The Neil Armstrong You Didn't Know" by Douglas Brinkley, *Newsweek* (September 10, 2012)

"Mission accomplished: Neil Armstrong is best known as the first man to walk on the moon.
But his finest day was aboard Gemini 8," *Maclean's* (September 10, 2012)

"Neil from Dullsville who fell to earth" by Janine di Giovanni, *Sunday Times* (London; July 10, 1994)

"Armstrong: A giant leap for modesty," *Christian Science Monitor* (August 27, 2012)

"Neil Armstrong, lunar explorer: the first moonwalker's brief lunar sojourn
yielded a scientific treasure trove," *Sky & Telescope* (December 2012)

Mission Control, This Is Apollo by Andrew Chaikin and Alan Bean (Viking Books for Young Readers, 2009)

FURTHER READING FOR KIDS

Who Was Neil Armstrong? by Roberta Edwards (Penguin Workshop, 2008)

One Giant Leap by Robert Burleigh (Philomel, 2009)

Moonshot by Brian Floca (Atheneum, 2009)

Hidden Figures (picture book edition) by Margot Lee Shetterly (HarperCollins, 2018)

· ·

DIAL BOOKS FOR YOUNG READERS
Penguin Young Readers Group • An imprint of Penguin Random House LLC • 375 Hudson Street, New York, NY 10014

Text copyright © 2018 by Forty-four Steps, Inc. • Illustrations copyright © 2018 by Christopher Eliopoulos

ISBN 9780735228726

Portrait of Neil Armstrong (page 38) and photo of Neil Armstrong standing on the moon's surface (page 39) courtesy of NASA.
Photo of three astronauts on page 39 courtesy of Bettmann/Getty Images. Photo of Strelka and Belka on page 39 courtesy of TASS/Getty Images.
Printed in China • 10 9 8 7 6 5 4 3 2 1
Designed by Jason Henry • Text set in Triplex • The artwork for this book was created digitally.

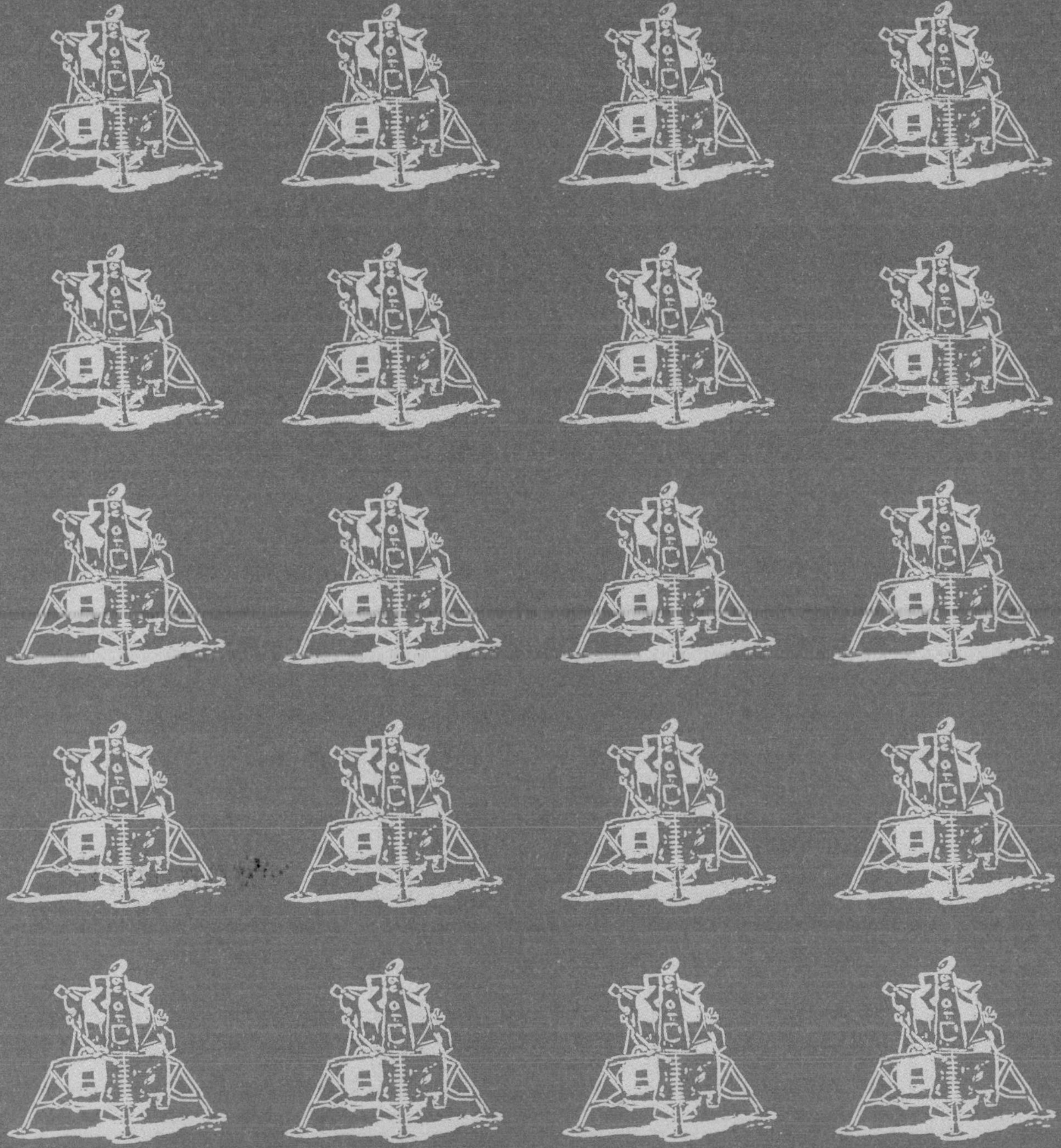

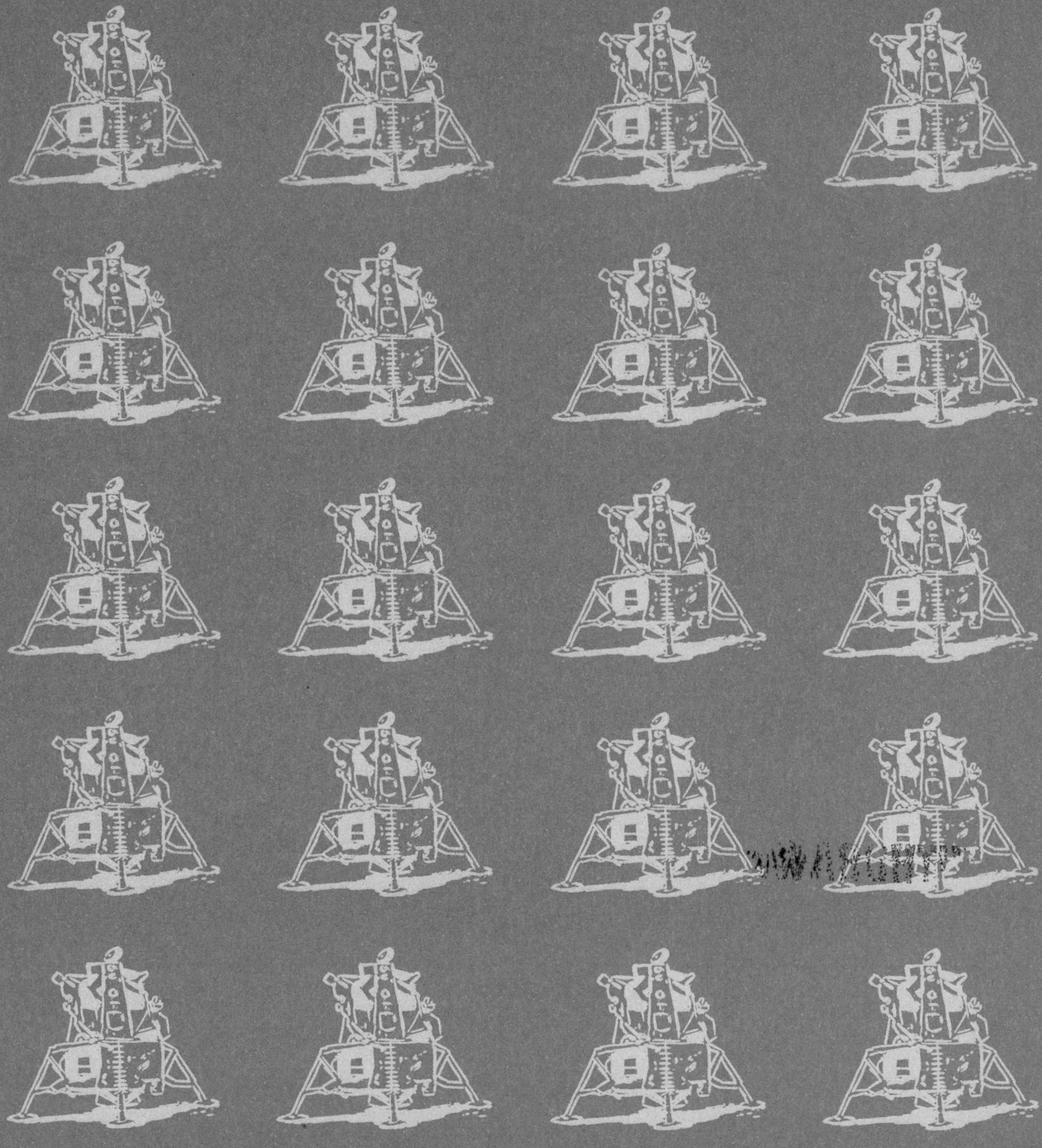